COLLINS
TRAVEL
GEM

PORTUGUESE

PHRASE BOOK

GW00367936

COLLINS
London and Glasgow

First published 1987

Consultant
Daniel Pires

ISBN 0 00 459407-X

Other Travel Gem
Phrase Books:

French

German

Spanish

Italian

Greek

Yugoslav

Your **Travel Gem** Phrase Book will prove an invaluable companion on your holiday or trip abroad. In a genuinely handy format, it gives you all you need to say for basic communication, with fast and direct alphabetical access to the relevant information. Be sure to pack it with your passport!

Its layout provides two means of quick alphabetical access:

> 99 practical topics arranged in A-to-Z order from ACCOMMODATION to WINE LIST via such topics as MENUS, ROOM SERVICE and TAXIS. Each topic gives you the basic phrases you will need, and in many cases an additional list with useful extra words. Just flick through the pages to the topic you need to look up;

> an alphabetical index at the back - WORDS - listing up to 1400 key words found in the 99 topics, for fast access to words which do not immediately seem to belong to a particular topic (such as 'safety pin, lose, passport').

This way you have the possibility of browsing through topics, as in more traditional phrase books, as well as having the advantage of alphabetical listing. The best of both worlds.

For information on GRAMMAR, PRONUNCIATION, the ALPHABET or CONVERSION CHARTS, just flick through the pages until you get to that topic in alphabetical order. Though **Travel Gems** do not assume prior knowledge of the foreign language, some basic facts about grammar will help you improvise and get more out of your conversations with local people.

Whenever relevant, travel information has been included. Some likely replies to what you might say have also been shown in several topics (such as DENTIST or DOCTOR).

Enjoy your stay!

You should carry a red warning triangle in case of breakdowns or accidents.

There's been an accident Houve um acidente
ohv oom aseedent

I've crashed my car Tive um choque com o meu carro
teev oom shok kong oo may-oo karroo

Can I see your insurance certificate? Posso ver o seu seguro?
possoo vehr oo say-oo suhgooroo

We will have to report it to the police Temos que comunicar à polícia
tay-moosh kuh koomoonee-kar a pooleess-yuh

He ran into me Ele chocou contra mim
ayl shookoh kontruh meeng

He was driving too fast Ele vinha em alta velocidade
ayl veen-yuh ayng altuh veloo-seedahd

He was too close Ele estava demasiado perto de mim
ayl shtah-vuh duh-muh-zee-ah-doo pehrtoo duh meeng

He did not give way Ele não deu prioridade
ayl nowng day-oo pree-oree-dahd

The car number was ... A matrícula do carro era ...
uh ma-treekooluh doo karroo ehruh ...

He was coming from my right/left Ele vinha da minha direita/esquerda
ayl veen-yuh duh meen-yuh deeray-tuh/shkehr-duh

damage
o prejuizo
prej-weezoo

documents
os documentos
dookoo-mentoosh

driving licence
a carta de condução
kartuh duh kondoo-sowng

green card
a carta verde
kartuh vehrd

insurance company
a companhia de seguros
kompan-yee-uh duh suh-gooroosh

law
a lei
lay

lawyer
o advogado
advoogah-doo

offence
a transgressão
tranj-gresowng

police station
a esquadra (da policia)
shkwah-druh (duh pooleess-yuh)

See also EMERGENCIES

Before you set off it is always advisable to obtain proper accident and medical insurance. Ambulances have to be paid for and the telephone number for an ambulance is 115.

There has been an accident Houve um acidente
ohv oom aseedent

Call an ambulance/a doctor Chame uma ambulância/um médico
shahm oomuh amboolanss-yuh/oom medikoo

He has hurt himself Ele feriu-se
ayl fer-yoo-suh

I am hurt Estou ferido
shtoh fereedoo

He is seriously injured/bleeding Ele está muito ferido/a sangrar
ayl shta mweentoo fereedoo/uh sangrar

He can't breathe/move Ele não pode respirar/mexer-se
ayl nowng pod rushperar/mushehr-suh

I can't move my arm/leg Não posso mexer o braço/a perna
nowng possoo mushehr oo brah-soo/uh pehr-nuh

Cover him up Cubram-no
koobrowng-noo

Don't move him Não lhe mexam
nowng l-yuh meshowng

He has broken his arm/cut himself Ele partiu o braço/cortou-se
ayl part-yoo oo brah-soo/koortoh-suh

I have had a fall Dei uma queda
day oomuh keduh

bandage a ligadura *leeguh-dooruh*	
bite, to morder *moordehr*	
dead morto *mortoo*	
dislocate, to deslocar *duj-lookar*	
hospital o hospital *oshpeetal*	
serious grave *grahv*	
slip, to escorregar *shkooruh-gar*	
sprain o deslocamento *duj-lookuh-mentoo*	
stung mordido *moordeedoo*	
sunburn a queimadura de sol *kaymuh-dooruh duh sol*	
sunstroke a insolação *eensooluh-sowng*	

See also HOTEL DESK, ROOM SERVICE, SELF-CATERING
Hotels are grouped into categories of one to five stars and
boarding houses (*pensões* and *albergues*) are graded one, two or
three stars. You can also stay in state-run luxury inns (*pousadas*)
which often are converted historical buildings in beautiful
settings.

I want to reserve a single/double room
Quero reservar um quarto individual/um
quarto de casal
*kehroo ruh-zervar oom kwartoo
eendeeveed-wal/oom kwartoo duh kazal*

Is there a restaurant/bar? Há um
restaurante/bar?
a oom rushtoh-rant/bar

**Do you have facilities for the
disabled?** Tem instalações para
deficientes?
*tayng een-shtalluh-soynsh paruh duh-
feess-yentsh*

I want bed and breakfast/full board
Quero dormida e pequeno almoço/pensão
completa
*kehroo door-meeduh ee puh-kaynoo
almoh-soo/pensowng kompletuh*

What is the daily/weekly rate? Qual é a
diária?/Quanto custa por semana?
*kwal e uh dee-ar-yuh/kwantoo kooshtuh
poor semah-nuh*

I want to stay three nights/from ... till
... Quero ficar três noites/do dia ... ao dia ...
*kehroo feekar traysh noytsh/doo dee-uh ...
ow dee-uh ...*

We'll be arriving at 7 p.m./very late
Vamos chegar às sete horas da
tarde/muito tarde
*vah-moosh shuh-gar ash set orush duh
tard/mweentoo tard*

balcony	a varanda
	varanduh
bathroom	a casa de banho
	kah-zuh duh bahn-yoo
double bed	a cama de casal
	kah-muh duh kazal
evening meal	o jantar
	jantar
half-board	a meia pensão
	mayuh pen-sowng
lift	o elevador
	eeluh-vuh-dor
lunch	o almoço
	almoh-soo
single bed	a cama de solteiro
	kah-muh duh soltay-roo
youth hostel	o albergue da juventude
	albehrg duh jooventood

Where do I check in for the flight to London? Onde faço o check-in para o voo de Londres?
onduh fah-soo oo check-in paruh oo voh-oo duh londrush

I'd like an aisle/a window seat Gostava de um lugar perto da coxia/da janela
gooshtah-vuh doom loogar pehrtoo duh kooshee-uh/duh janeluh

Will a meal be served on the plane? Vão servir uma refeição no avião?
vowng serveer oomuh ruh-fay-sowng noo av-yowng

Where is the snack bar/duty-free shop? Onde fica o snack-bar/a free-shop?
onduh feekuh oo snack-bar/uh free-shop

Where can I change some money? Onde posso cambiar dinheiro?
onduh possoo kamb-yar deen-yay-roo

Where do I get the bus to town? Onde se apanha o autocarro para a cidade?
onduh see apahn-yuh oo owtoo-karroo pra seedahd

Where are the taxis/telephones? Onde ficam os táxis/os telefones?
onduh feekowng oosh taxeesh/oosh tuh-luh-fonsh

I want to hire a car/reserve a hotel room Quero alugar um carro/reservar um quarto
kehroo aloogar oom karroo/ruh-zervar oom kwartoo

I am being met Estão à minha espera
shtowng a meen-yuh shpehruh

airport o aeroporto
uh-ehroo-portoo

baggage reclaim o tapete rolante
tapet roolant

check-in desk o balcão do check-in
balkowng doo check-in

land, to aterrar
uh-terar

lounge a sala de espera
sah-luh duh shpehruh

non-smoking não fumadores
nowng foomuh-dorush

passport control o controle de passaportes
kontrol duh passuh-portsh

The Portuguese alphabet is the same as the English one, with the exception of three letters: K, W and Y. These letters are used with foreign words that have come into use in Portuguese.

A como	**Alexandre**			**N** como	**Nicolau**	
a *koh-moo*	aluh-*shandruh*			en *koh-moo*	neekoo-*la-oo*	
B	**Banana**			**O**	**Óscar**	
bay	banah-nuh			oh	oshkar	
C	**Carlos**			**P**	**Paris**	
say	karloosh			pay	pareesh	
D	**Daniel**			**Q**	**Quarto**	
day	dan-yel			kay	kwartoo	
E	**Eduardo**			**R**	**Ricardo**	
ay	eedwardoo			err	reekardoo	
F	**França**			**S**	**Susana**	
ef	fransuh			ess	soozanuh	
G	**Gabriel**			**T**	**Teresa**	
jay	gabree-el			tay	tuh-ray-zuh	
H	**Holanda**			**U**	**Ulisses**	
aga	oh-landuh			oo	ooleesush	
I	**Itália**			**V**	**Venezuela**	
ee	eetal-yuh			vay	vuh-nuh-zway-luh	
J	**José**					
jotuh	jooze			**X**	**Xangai**	
L	**Lisboa**			sheesh	shang-gye	
el	leejboh-uh			**Z**	**Zebra**	
M	**Maria**			zay	zebruh	
em	maree-uh					

Is it far/expensive? Fica longe?/É caro?
feekuh lonj/e kah-roo

Are you ...? É você ...?
e voh-se ...

Do you understand? Compreende?
kompree-end

Can I go in there? Posso lá entrar?
possoo la ayn-trar

Can you help me? Pode ajudar-me?
pod ajoodar-muh

Where is the chemist's? Onde fica a farmácia?
onduh feekuh uh farmass-yuh

Where are the toilets? Onde é a casa de banho?
ondee e uh kah-zuh duh bahn-yoo

When will it be ready? Quando é que está pronto?
kwandoo e kuh shta pront

How do I get there? Como se vai para lá?
koh-moo suh vy paruh la

How far/big is it ? A que distância fica?/Que tamanho tem?
uh kuh deesh-tanss-yuh feekuh/kuh taman-yoo tayng

Is there a good restaurant? Há um bom restaurante?
a oom bong rushtoh-rant

What is this? O que é isto?
oo kee e eeshtoo

Which is your room? Qual é o seu quarto?
kwal e oo say-oo kwartoo

Who is coming? Quem é que vem?
kayng e kuh vayng

How much is it? Quanto custa?
kwantoo kooshtuh

How many kilometres? Quantos kilómetros?
kwantoosh kee-lometroosh

Is this the bus for ...? É este o autocarro para ...?
e aysht oo owtoo-karroo paruh ...

A red flag on a Portuguese beach means that it is dangerous to go swimming. A yellow flag means that you can swim, but it is not recommended. If you see a green flag, go right ahead!

Is it safe to swim here? Não há perigo de nadar aqui?
nowng a pereegoo duh nadar akee

When is high/low tide? Quando é a maré-alta/a maré-baixa?
kwandoo e uh mare-altuh/uh mare-by-shuh

Is the water deep? É fundo?
e foondoo

Are there strong currents? Há correntes fortes?
a koo-rentsh fortsh

Is it a private/quiet beach? É uma praia particular/sossegada?
e oomuh pry-uh parteekoo-lar/soo-suh-gah-duh

Where do we change? Onde é que nos mudamos?
ondee e kuh noosh moodah-moosh

Can I hire a deck chair/boat? Posso alugar uma cadeira de lona/um barco?
possoo aloogar oomuh kaday-ruh duh lonuh/oom barkoo

Can I go fishing/windsurfing? Posso ir pescar/fazer windsurf?
possoo eer pushkar/fazehr windsurf

Is there a children's pool? Há uma piscina para crianças?
a oomuh peesh-seenuh paruh kree-ansush

Where can I get an ice-cream? Onde é que há gelados?
ondee e kee a jelah-doosh

armbands
as braçadeiras
brassuh-day-rush

bucket
o balde
balduh

lifeguard
o nadador salvador
naduh-dor salvuh-dor

sea
o mar
mar

spade
a pá
pa

sunglasses
os óculos de sol
okooloosh duh sol

sunshade
o guarda-sol
gwarduh-sol

suntan oil
o bronzeador
bronzee-uh-dor

swimsuit
o fato de banho
fah-too duh bahn-yoo

towel
a toalha
too-al-yuh

BODY

ankle
o tornozelo
toornoo-__zel__oo

arm
o braço
brah-soo

back
as costas
koshtush

body
o corpo
korpoo

bone
o osso
ossoo

breast
o peito
pay-too

buttocks
as nâdegas
nad__uh__-gush

cheek
a face
fass

chest
o peito
pay-too

ear
a orelha
oh-__rel__-yuh

elbow
o cotovelo
koh-too-__vel__oo

eye
o olho
__ohl__-yoo

face
a cara
__kah__-ruh

finger
o dedo
day-doo

foot
o pé
pe

hand
a mão
mowng

head
a cabeça
kabay-suh

heart
o coração
kooruh-__sowng__

joint
a articulação
ar-teekooluh-__sowng__

kidney
o rim
reeng

knee
o joelho
joo-__el__-yoo

leg
a perna
pehrnuh

liver
o fígado
__feeg__uh-doo

lung
o pulmão
pool-__mowng__

mouth
a boca
boh-kuh

muscle
o músculo
__moosh__-kooloo

neck
o pescoço
push-__koh__-soo

nose
o nariz
nar__eesh__

shoulder
o ombro
__ombr__oo

skin
a pele
pel

stomach
o estômago
__shtoh__-magoo

throat
a garganta
gargantuh

thumb
o polegar
pohluh-__gar__

toe
o dedo do pé
__day__-doo doo pe

tongue
a lingua
__leeng__-wuh

wrist
o pulso
__pool__soo

My car has broken down O meu carro avariou-se
*oo **may**-oo **karroo** avaree-**oh**-suh*

There is something wrong with the brakes Os travões não funcionam bem
*oosh travoynsh nowng foonsee-**onowng** bayng*

I have run out of petrol Acabou-se-me a gasolina
*akuh-**boh**-suh-muh uh gazoo-**lee**nuh*

There is a leak in the radiator/petrol tank Há uma ruptura no radiador/depósito da gasolina
*a **oomuh** rooptooruh noo radee-uh-**dor**/duh-**pozi**too duh gazoo-**lee**nuh*

The engine is overheating O motor aquece demais
*oo moo**tor** akess duh-**mysh***

Can you tow me to a garage? Pode rebocar-me para uma garagem?
*pod ruh-boo**kar**-muh **proo**muh garah-jayng*

Can you send a mechanic/a breakdown van? Pode mandar um mecânico/um pronto socorro?
*pod man**dar** oom muh-**kahni**koo/oom pront soo**korro**oo*

Do you have the parts? Tem as peças?
*tayng ush **pess**ush*

The windscreen has shattered O pára-brisas partiu-se
*oo para-**bree**zush pert-**yoo**-suh*

Can you do a temporary repair? Pode fazer uma reparação temporária?
*pod fa**zehr** **oo**muh ruh-para**sowng** tempoo-**rar**-yuh*

bulb a lâmpada
lahm-puh-duh

emergency windscreen o pára-brisas de emergência
*paruh-**bree**zush deemer-**jenss**-yuh*

flat tyre o furo
fooroo

hazard lights as luzes de perigo
loozush duh pereegoo

jack o macaco
makah-koo

jump leads os cabos de emergência
kah-boosh deemer-jenss-yuh

spanner a chave de parafusos
shahv duh paruh-foozoosh

tow rope o cabo de reboque
kah-boo duh ruh-bok

warning triangle o triângulo
tree-angooloo

wheel brace a chave de roda
shahv duh roduh

I have an appointment with ... Tenho um encontro com ...
ten-yoo oom ayng-kontroo kong ...

He is expecting me Ele está à minha espera
ayl shta a meen-yuh shpehruh

Can I leave a message with his secretary? Posso deixar um recado à secretária?
possoo day-shar oom rekah-doo a sekruh-tar-yuh

I am free tomorrow morning/for lunch Estou livre amanhã de manhã/para almoçar
shtoh leevruh amanyang duh manyang/paruh almoosar

Here is my business card Aqui tem o meu cartão
akee tayng oo may-oo kartowng

Can I send a telex from here? Posso mandar um telex daqui?
possoo mandar oom telex dakee

Where can I get some photocopying done? Onde é que eu posso fazer fotocópias?
ondee e kee ay-oo possoo fazehr footoo-kop-yush

I want to send this by courier Quero mandar isto por um mensageiro
kehroo mandar eeshtoo poor oom mensa-jay-roo

I will send you further details/a sample Vou-lhe mandar mais pormenores/uma amostra
voh-l-yuh mandar mysh poormuh-norush/oomuh amosh-truh

Have you a catalogue/some literature? Tem um catálogo/ instruções?
tayng oom ka-taloogoo/een-shtroo-soynsh

I am going to the trade fair/the exhibition Vou à feira das indústrias/à exposição
voh a fayruh duz eendoosh-tree-ush/a shpoozee-sowng

See also COLOURS AND SHAPES, DESCRIBING THINGS, MEASUREMENTS AND QUANTITIES, PAYING, SHOPPING

Do you sell stamps? Vende selos?
vend say-loosh

How much is that? Quanto custa?
kwantoo kooshtuh

Have you anything bigger/smaller?
Tem maior/mais pequeno?
tayng ma-yor/mysh puh-kay-noo

Have you got any bread/matches? Tem
pão/fósforos?
tayng powng/fosh-fooroosh

I'd like a newspaper/some apples
Quero um jornal/maçãs
kehroo oom joornal/masansh

A packet of cigarettes please Um maço
de cigarros, por favor
oom mah-soo duh see-garroosh poor favor

I prefer this one Prefiro este
pruh-feeroo aysht

I'd like to see the one in the window
Quero ver aquele que está na montra
kehroo vehr akayl kuh shta nuh montruh

I'll take this one/that one there Levo
este/aquele
levoo aysht/akayl

Could you wrap it up for me please?
Pode embrulhar, por favor?
pod aymbrool-yar poor favor

**I think you've given me the wrong
change** Acho que o troco não está certo
ashoo kee oo trokoo nowng shta sehr-too

100 grammes of
cem gramas de
saying grah-mush duh

a kilo of
um quilo de
oom keeloo duh

cheaper
mais barato
mysh barah-too

department
a secção
seksowng

department store
o grande armazém
grand armuh-zayng

expensive
caro
kah-roo

shop
a loja
lojuh

supermarket
o supermercado
sooper-merkah-doo

Portugal has many official campsites and all provide the full range of facilities. You are advised to use these and not camp anywhere else without permission.

We are looking for a campsite
Procuramos um parque de campismo
prookoo-rah-mooz oom park duh kam-peej-moo

Do you have any vacancies? Tem lugares vagos?
tayng loogah-rush vah-goosh

How much is it per night? Quanto custa por noite?
kwantoo kooshtuh poor noyt

We want to stay one night Queremos ficar uma noite
kray-moosh feekar oomuh noyt

May we camp here? Podemos acampar aqui?
pooday-moosh akampar akee

Can we park our caravan there?
Podemos estacionar a caravana ali?
pooday-moosh shtass-yoonar uh karavah-nuh alee

Is there a shop/restaurant? Há alguma loja/algum restaurante?
a algoomuh lojuh/algoom rushtoh-rant

Where is the washroom? Onde fica a casa de banho?
onduh feekuh uh kah-zuh duh bahn-yoo

What facilities do you have on the site? Que instalações tem o parque de campismo?
kuh een-shtaluh-soynsh tayng oo park duh kam-peej-moo

Is there electricity on site? Há electricidade no parque de campismo?
a eele-treesee-dahd noo park duh kam-peej-moo

air-mattress	o colchão pneumático *kolshowng nay-oomatikoo*
camp-bed	a cama de campismo *kah-muh duh kampeejmoo*
fly sheet	o tecto duplo *tetoo dooploo*
gas cylinder	a botija de gás *booteejuh duh gash*
guy rope	a espia *shpee-uh*
mallet	o maço *mah-soo*
sleeping bag	o saco cama *sah-koo kah-muh*
tent	a tenda *tenduh*
tent peg	a estaca *shtah-kuh*
tent pole	o mastro da tenda *mashtroo duh tenduh*
trailer	o atrelado *atruh-lah-doo*

I want to hire a car Quero alugar um carro
kehroo aloogar oom karroo

I need a car with a chauffeur Preciso de um carro com
condutor
pre-seezoo doom karroo kong kondootor

I want a large/small car Quero um carro grande/pequeno
kehroo oom karroo grand/puh-kaynoo

Is there a charge per km? Há alguma taxa por quilómetro?
a algoomuh tashuh poor kee-lometroo

How much extra is the comprehensive insurance cover?
Quanto é que tenho que pagar mais para ter um seguro contra
todos os riscos?
*kwantoo e kuh ten-yoo kuh pagar mysh paruh tehr oom
segooroo kontruh toh-dooz oosh reeshkoosh*

I would like to leave the car in Lisbon Gostava de deixar o
carro em Lisboa
gooshtah-vuh duh day-shar oo karroo ayng leej-boh-uh

My husband/wife will be driving as well O meu marido/a
minha mulher também vai conduzir
*oo may-oo mareedoo/uh meen-yuh mool-yehr tambayng vy
kondoo-zeer*

Is there a radio/radio-cassette? Tem telefonia/gravador?
tayng tuh-luh-foonee-uh/gravuh-dor

How do I operate the controls? Como funcionam os
comandos do carro?
koh-moo foonss-yonowng oosh koo-mandoosh doo karroo

Please explain the car documents Por favor, explique-me
quais são os documentos do carro
*poor favor shpleek-muh kwysh sowng oosh dookoo-mentoosh
doo karroo*

accelerator
o acelerador
assuh-luh-ruh-dor

alternator
o alternador
altehr-nuh-dor

automatic
automático
owtoo-matikoo

battery
a bateria
batuh-ree-uh

bonnet
o capot
kapoh

boot
o porta-bagagens
portuh-bagah-jaynsh

brake fluid
o óleo dos travões
*ol-yoo doosh
travoynsh*

brakes
os travões
travoynsh

carburettor
o carburador
karbooruh-dor

choke
o ar
ar

clutch
a embraiagem
aym-bry-ah-jayng

distributor
o distribuidor
deeshtreeb-weedor

dynamo
o dínamo
deenamoo

engine
o motor
mootor

exhaust pipe
o tubo de escape
tooboo dushkap

fan belt
a correia da
ventoinha
*koorayuh duh
ventoo-een-yuh*

fuse
o fusível
foozeevel

gears
as mudanças
moodansush

handbrake
o travão de mão
*travowng duh
mowng*

headlights
os faróis
faroysh

hose
o tubo
tooboo

ignition
a ignição
eegnee-sowng

indicator
o pisca-pisca
*peeshkuh-
peeshkuh*

points
os platinados
plateenah-doosh

radiator
o radiador
radee-uh-dor

reversing lights
as luzes de
marcha-atrás
*loozush duh
marshuh-atrash*

shock absorber
o amortecedor
amor-tussuh-dor

spark plugs
as velas
velush

steering
a direcção
dee-re-sowng

steering wheel
o volante
voolant

tyre
o pneu
pnay-oo

wheel
a roda
roduh

windscreen
o pára-brisas
paruh-breezush

**windscreen
washer**
o lava pára-brisas
*lavuh paruh-
breezush*

**windscreen
wiper**
o limpa pára-brisas
*leempuh paruh-
breezush*

See also PUBLIC HOLIDAYS

When are the local festivals? Quando são as festas locais?
kwandoo sowng ush feshtush lookysh

Happy birthday! Parabéns!
paruh-baynsh

Merry Christmas! Feliz Natal!
fuh-leesh nuh-tal

Happy New Year! Bom Ano Novo!
bong ah-noo noh-voo

Congratulations! Parabéns!
paruh-baynsh

Best wishes for ... Os meus melhores votos para ...
ooj may-oosh mul-yorush votoosh paruh ...

Have a good time! Divirta-se!
deeveer-tuh-suh

Cheers! Saúde!
suh-ood

Enjoy your meal! Bom proveito!
bong proo-vaytoo

baptism
o baptismo
bateejmoo

holiday
as férias
fehr-yush

party
a festa
feshtuh

public holiday
o feriado
fuh-ree-ah-doo

wedding
o casamento
kazuh-mentoo

I want something for a headache/sore throat/toothache Quero qualquer coisa para as dores de cabeça/de garganta/ de dentes
kehroo kwal-kehr koyzuh prash dorush duh kabay-suh/duh gargantuh/duh dentsh

I would like some aspirin/sticking plaster Quero aspirinas/pensos
kehroo ashpee-reenush/pensoosh

Have you anything for insect bites/ sunburn/diarrhoea? Tem alguma coisa para as mordeduras de insectos/as queimaduras/a diarreia?
tayng algoomuh koyzuh prash morduh-doorush deen-sektoosh/ush kaymuh-doorush/uh dee-uh-rayuh

I have a cold/a cough Estou constipado/ Tenho tosse
shtoh kon-shteepah-doo/ten-yoo tohss

Is this suitable for an upset stomach/ hay fever? Isto é bom para as dores de estômago/a febre dos fenos?
eeshtoo e bong prash dorush dushtoh-muh-goo/uh februh doosh fay-noosh

How much/how many do I take? Quanto/quantos tomo?
kwantoo/kwantoosh tomoo

How often do I take it? Quantas vezes o tomo?
kwantush vay-zuz oo tomoo

Is it safe for children? Não há perigo para as crianças?
nowng a pereegoo prash kree-ansush

How do I get reimbursed? Como é que posso ser reembolsado?
koh-moo e kuh possoo sehr ree-aymbol-sah-doo

antiseptic
o antiséptico
antee-septikoo

bandage
a ligadura
leeguh-dooruh

contraceptive
o contraceptivo
kontruh-septeevoo

cotton wool
o algodão em rama
algoodowng ayng rah-muh

cream
o creme
krem

insect repellant
o repelente
ruh-puh-lent

laxative
o laxativo
lashuh-teevoo

lotion
a loção
loh-sowng

prescription
a receita
ruh-say-tuh

sanitary towels
os pensos higiénicos
pensoosh eej-yenikoosh

tampons
os tampões
tampoynsh

I have two children Tenho duas crianças
ten-yoo doo-ush kree-ansush

Do you have a special rate for children? Há um preço especial para crianças?
a oom pray-soo shpuss-yal paruh kree-ansush

Do you have facilities for children? Tem instalações para crianças?
tayng een-shtaluh-soynsh paruh kree-ansush

Have you got a cot for the baby? Tem um berço para o bebé?
tayng oom behr-soo pro bebe

Do you have a special menu for children? Tem uma ementa especial para crianças?
tayng oomuh eementuh shpuss-yal paruh kree-ansush

Where can I feed/change the baby? Onde é que posso dar de comer ao bebé/mudar o bebé?
ondee e kuh possoo dar duh koomehr ow bebe/moodar oo bebe

Where can I warm the baby's bottle? Onde é que posso aquecer o biberão do bebé?
ondee e kuh possoo akesehr oo beebuh-rowng doo bebe

Is there a playroom? Há uma sala infantil?
a oomuh sah-luh eemfanteel

Is there a babysitting service? Há alguém que tome conta dos bebés?
a algayng kuh tom kontuh doosh bebesh

My son is six years old O meu filho tem seis anos
oo may-oo feel-yoo tayng sayz ah-noosh

activities
as actividades
ateevee-dah-dush

baby food
a comida para bebé
koomeeduh paruh bebe

babysitter
a babysitter
babysitter

boy
o rapaz
rapash

disposable nappies
as fraldas descartáveis
fraldush dushkartah-vaysh

dummy
a chupeta
shoopetuh

girl
a rapariga
ruh-puh-reeguh

high chair
a cadeira de bebé
kaday-ruh duh bebe

nappy
a fralda
fralduh

pram
o carro de bebé
karroo duh bebe

push chair
a cadeira de bebé
kaday-ruh duh bebe

Where is the nearest church? Onde fica
a igreja mais próxima?
*onduh **feekuh** uh ee-**grejuh** mysh
prosseemuh*

Where is there a Protestant church?
Onde é que há uma igreja protestante?
*onduh e kee a **oomuh** ee-**grejuh** prootush-
tant*

I want to see a priest Quero falar com
um padre
kehroo** falar kong oom **padruh

What time is the service? A que horas é
a missa?
*uh kee oruz e uh **meessuh***

I want to go to confession Quero-me
confessar
***kehroo*-muh komfesar**

altar
o altar
altar

candle
a vela
veluh

cathedral
a catedral
*katuh-**dral***

Catholic
católico
katolikoo

chapel
a capela
kapeluh

churchyard
o adro
ah-droo

mass
a missa
mee-suh

minister
o pastor
pashtor

mosque
a mesquita
*mush-**keetuh***

rabbi
o rabino
rabeenoo

synagogue
a sinagoga
*seenuh-**goguh***

Does this bus/train go to ...? Este
autocarro/comboio vai para ... ?
*aysht owtoo-karroo/kom-boyoo vy
paruh ...*

Which number bus goes to ...? Qual é o
número do autocarro que vai para ... ?
*kwal e oo noomeroo doo owtoo-karroo
kuh vy paruh ...*

Where do I get a bus for the airport?
Onde é que posso apanhar o autocarro
para o aeroporto?
*ondee e kuh possoo apan-yar oo owtoo-
karroo pro uh-ehroo-portoo*

Which bus do I take for the museum?
Qual é o autocarro que vai para o museu?
*kwal e oo owtoo-karroo kuh vy pro
moozayoo*

Where do I change/get off? Onde é que
mudo/desço?
ondee e kuh moodoo/desh-soo

**Where is the nearest underground
station?** Onde fica a estação de metro
mais próxima?
*onduh feek ushta-sowng duh metroo mysh
prossimuh*

What is the fare to the town centre?
Quanto custa o bilhete para o centro da
cidade?
*kwantoo kooshtuh oo béel-yet pro
sentroo duh seedahd*

Where do I buy a ticket? Onde é que
compro um bilhete?
ondee e kuh komproo oom beel-yet

What time is the last bus? A que horas
é o último autocarro?
uh kee oruz e oo ooltimoo owtoo-karroo

book of tickets
a caderneta de
bilhetes
*kader-netuh duh
beel-yetsh*

bus stop
a paragem de
autocarro
*parah-jayng
dowtoo-karroo*

conductor
o cobrador
koobruh-dor

driver
o motorista
mootoo-reesh-tuh

escalator
a escada rolante
shkah-duh roolant

half fare
meio bilhete
mayoo beel-yet

lift
o elevador
eeluh-vuh-dor

season ticket
o passe
pass

tourist ticket
o bilhete turístico
*beel-yet too-
reeshtikoo*

underground
o metropolitano
*metroo-pooleetah-
noo*

Is there a laundry service? Há um
serviço de lavandaria?
a oom ser-veesoo duh lavanduh-ree-uh

**Is there a launderette/dry cleaner's
nearby?** Há uma lavandaria/limpeza a
seco aqui perto?
*a oomuh lavanduh-ree-uh/leempay-zuh uh
say-koo akee pehrtoo*

**Where can I get this skirt cleaned/
ironed?** Onde é que posso mandar
limpar/passar a ferro esta saia?
*ondee e kuh possoo mandar
leempar/pasar uh ferroo eshtuh sy-uh*

I need to wash this off immediately
Preciso de tirar isto urgentemente
*pre-seezoo duh teerar eeshtoo oorjent-
ment*

Where can I do some washing? Onde é
que posso lavar a roupa?
ondee e kuh possoo lavar uh roh-puh

I need some soap and water Preciso de
sabão e água
pre-seezoo duh sabowng ee ahg-wuh

Where can I dry my clothes? Onde é
que posso secar a roupa?
ondee e kuh possoo sekar uh roh-puh

This stain is coffee/blood Esta nódoa é
de café/sangue
eshtuh nod-wuh e duh kuh-fe/sanguh

Can you remove this stain? Pode tirar
esta nódoa?
pod teerar eshtuh nod-wuh

It is very delicate É muito delicado
e mweentoo duh-lee-kah-doo

When will my things be ready?
Quando é que está pronto?
kwandoo e kuh shta pront

disinfectant
o desinfectante
duzeen-fektant

laundry room
a lavandaria
lavanduh-ree-uh

sink
o lava-louça
lavuh-loh-suh

tap
a torneira
toornay-ruh

washbasin
o lavatório
lavuh-tor-yoo

washing powder
o detergente
duh-ter-jent

washroom
a casa de banho
kah-zuh duh bahn-yoo

I take a continental size 40 O meu
número é o quarenta
oo mayoo noomeroo e oo kwarentuh

Can you measure me, please? Pode
medir-me, por favor?
pod medeer-muh poor favor

May I try on this dress? Posso
experimentar este vestido?
possoo shpuh-reementar aysht vush-teedoo

May I take it over to the light? Posso
vê-lo à luz?
possoo veh-loo a loosh

Where are the changing rooms? Onde
ficam os gabinetes de provas?
*onduh feekowng oosh gabee-netsh duh
provush*

Is there a mirror? Há um espelho?
a oom shpel-yoo

It's too big/small Fica-me muito
grande/pequeno
feekuh-muh mweentoo grand/puh-kay-noo

What is the material? Qual é a fazenda?
kwal e uh fazenduh

Is it washable? É lavável?
e lavah-vel

I don't like it Não gosto
nowng goshtoo

I don't like the colour Não gosto da cor
nowng goshtoo duh kor

belt
o cinto
seentoo

blouse
a blusa
bloozuh

bra
o soutien
soot-yang

button
o botão
bootowng

cardigan
o casaco de malha
*kazah-koo duh
mal-yuh*

clothes
a roupa
roh-puh

coat
o casaco
kazah-koo

cotton
o algodão
algoo-downg

denim
a ganga
ganguh

dress
o vestido
vush-teedoo

fabric
o tecido
tuh-seedoo

fur
a pele
pel

gloves
as luvas
loovush

hat
o chapéu
shapay-oo

jacket
o casaco
kazah-koo

jeans
as jeans
jeans

lace
o atacador
atakuh-dor

leather
o couro
koh-roo

nightdress
a camisa de noite
kameezuh duh noyt

nylon
o nylon
neelon

panties
as cuecas de
senhora
*kwekush duh sun-
yoruh*

pants
as cuecas
kwekush

petticoat
a combinação
kombeenuh-sowng

polyester
o poliéster
poolee-eshter

pyjamas
o pijama
peejah-muh

raincoat
a gabardina
gabar-deenuh

sandals
as sandálias
san-dahl-yush

scarf
o cachecol
kashuh-kol

shirt
a camisa
kamee-zuh

shoes
os sapatos
sapah-toosh

shorts
os calções
kal-soynsh

silk
a seda
seduh

skirt
a saia
sy-uh

socks
as meias
mayush

stockings
as meias de
senhora
*mayush duh sun-
yoruh*

suede
a camurça
kamoorsuh

suit (man's)
o fato
fah-too

suit (woman's)
o fato
fah-too

sweater
a camisola
kamee-zoluh

swimsuit
o fato de banho
*fah-too duh bahn-
yoo*

t-shirt
a t-shirt
t-shirt

tie
a gravata
gravah-tuh

tights
os collants
koolansh

trousers
as calças
kalsush

trunks
os calções de banho
*kalsoynsh duh
bahn-yoo*

vest
a camisola interior
*kamee-zoluh
eentuh-ree-or*

wool
a lã
lang

zip
o fecho éclair
feshoo ay-klehr

Is there a bus to ...? Há algum autocarro
para ...?
a algoom owtoo-karroo paruh ...

Which bus goes to ...? Qual é o autocarro
que vai para ...?
kwal e oo owtoo-karroo kuh vy paruh ...

Where do I catch the bus for ...? Onde é
que posso apanhar o autocarro para ...?
*ondee e kuh posso apan-yar oo owtoo-
karroo paruh ...*

What are the times of the buses to ...?
A que horas partem os autocarros para ...?
*uh kee orush partayng ooz owtoo-
karroosh paruh ...*

Does this bus go to ...? Este autocarro vai
para ...?
aysht owtoo-karroo vy paruh ...

Where do I get off? Onde é que desço?
ondee e kuh desh-soo

Is there a toilet on board? O autocarro
tem casa de banho?
*oo owtoo-karroo tayng kah-zuh duh bahn-
yoo*

Is there an overnight service to ...? Há
um autocarro à noite para ...?
a oom owtoo-karroo a noyt paruh ...

What time does it leave? A que horas é
que parte?
uh kee oruz e kuh part

What time does it arrive? A que horas é
que chega?
uh kee oruz e kuh shay-guh

Will you tell me where to get off?
Pode-me dizer onde é que desço?
pod-muh dee-zehr ondee e kuh desh-soo

bus depot
a estação de
autocarros
*shta-sowng
dowtoo-karroosh*

driver
o motorista
mootoo-reeshtuh

film show
com projecção de
filmes
*kong proo-je-
sowng duh feelmsh*

luggage hold
o porta-bagagens
*portuh-bagah-
jaynsh*

luggage rack
a rede
red

seat
o lugar
loogar

beige
bege
bej

big
grande
grand

black
preto
pray-too

blue
azul
azool

brown
castanho
kash-tahn-yoo

circular
circular
seerkoo-lar

crimson
carmesim
karmuh-zeeng

cube
o cubo
kooboo

dark
escuro
shkooroo

fat
gordo
gordoo

gold
dourado
doh-rah-doo

green
verde
vehrd

grey
cinzento
seenzentoo

lemon
amarelo claro
amuh-reloo klah-roo

light
claro
klah-roo

long
comprido
kompreedoo

mauve
violeta
vee-ooletuh

oblong
rectangular
retangoo-lar

orange
cor de laranja
kor duh laran-juh

oval
oval
oh-val

pink
cor-de-rosa
kor duh rozuh

pointed
ponteagudo
pontee-agoodoo

purple
roxo
roh-shoo

red
encarnado
ayng-karnah-doo

round
redondo
ruh-dondoo

shade
o tom
tong

shiny
brilhante
breel-yant

silver
prateado
pratee-ah-doo

small
pequeno
puh-kay-noo

square
quadrado
kwadrah-doo

thick
grosso
grossoo

thin
magro
mah-groo

tinted
colorido
kooloo-reedoo

turquoise
azul turquesa
azool toorkay-zuh

white
branco
brankoo

yellow
amarelo
amuh-reloo

This does not work Isto não funciona
eeshtoo nowng foonss-yonuh

I can't turn the heating off/on Não consigo desligar/ligar o aquecimento
nowng konseegoo duj-leegar/leegar oo akussee-mentoo

The lock is broken A fechadura está partida
uh feshuh-dooruh shta par-teeduh

I can't open the window Não posso abrir a janela
nowng possoo abreer uh janeluh

The toilet won't flush O autoclismo não trabalha
oo owtoo-kleej-moo nowng trabal-yuh

There is no hot water/toilet paper Não há água quente/papel higiénico
nowng a ahg-wuh kent/papel eej-yenikoo

The washbasin is dirty O lavatório está sujo
oo lavuh-tor-yoo shta soojoo

The room is noisy O quarto é barulhento
oo kwartoo e barool-yentoo

My coffee is cold O meu café está frio
oo may-oo kuh-fe shta free-oo

We are still waiting to be served Ainda estamos à espera que nos sirvam
a-eenduh shtah-mooz a shpehruh kuh noosh seervowng

I bought this here yesterday Comprei isto aqui ontem
kompray eeshtoo akee ontayng

It has a flaw/hole in it Tem um defeito/um buraco
tayng oom duh-fay-too/oom boorah-koo

How do you do? Como está?
koh-moo shta

Hello Olá
oh-la

Goodbye Adeus
aday-oosh

Do you speak English? Fala inglês?
fah-luh eenglesh

I don't speak Portuguese Não falo português
nowng fah-loo poortoo-gesh

What's your name? Como se chama?
koh-moo suh shah-muh

My name is ... Chamo-me ...
shah-moo-muh ...

Do you mind if I sit here? Importa-se se eu me sentar aqui?
eemportuh-suh see ay-oo muh sentar akee

I'm English/Scottish/Welsh Sou inglês/escocês/galês
soh eenglesh/shkoosesh/galesh

Are you Portuguese? É português?
e poortoo-gesh

Would you like to come out with me? Quer sair comigo?
kehr suh-eer koomeegoo

Yes, I should like to Sim, gostava
seeng gooshtah-vuh

No, thank you Não, obrigado
nowng oh-breegah-doo

Yes please Sim, por favor
seeng poor favor

No thank you Não, obrigado
nowng oh-breegah-doo

Thank you (very much) (Muito) obrigado
(mweent) oh-breegah-doo

Don't mention it Não tem importância
nowng tayng eempoor-tanss-yuh

I'm sorry Desculpe
dushkoolp

I'm on holiday here Estou aqui de férias
shtoh akee duh fehr-yush

This is my first trip to ... Esta é a minha primeira viagem a ...
eshtuh e uh meen-yuh preemay-ruh vee-ah-jayng uh ...

Do you mind if I smoke? Importa-se se eu fumar?
eemportuh-suh see ay-oo foomar

Would you like a drink? Quer uma bebida?
kehr oomuh bebeeduh

Have you ever been to Britain? Já foi à Grã-Bretanha?
ja foy a grambruh-tahn-yuh

Did you like it there? Gostou de lá estar?
goosh-toh duh la shtar

What part of Portugal are you from? De que parte de Portugal é?
duh kuh part duh poortoo-gal e

CONVERSION CHARTS 28

In the weight and length charts, the middle figure can be either metric or imperial. Thus 3.3 feet = 1 metre, 1 foot = 0.3 metres, and so on.

feet	metres		inches		cm	lbs		kg
3.3	1	0.3	0.39	1	2.54	2.2	1	0.45
6.6	2	0.61	0.79	2	5.08	4.4	2	0.91
9.9	3	0.91	1.18	3	7.62	6.6	3	1.4
13.1	4	1.22	1.57	4	10.6	8.8	4	1.8
16.4	5	1.52	1.97	5	12.7	11	5	2.2
19.7	6	1.83	2.36	6	15.2	13.2	6	2.7
23	7	2.13	2.76	7	17.8	15.4	7	3.2
26.2	8	2.44	3.15	8	20.3	17.6	8	3.6
29.5	9	2.74	3.54	9	22.9	19.8	9	4.1
32.9	10	3.05	3.9	10	25.4	22	10	4.5
			4.3	11	27.9			
			4.7	12	30.1			

°C	0	5	10	15	17	20	22	24	26	28	30	35	37	38	40	50	100
°F	32	41	50	59	63	68	72	75	79	82	86	95	98.4	100	104	122	212

Km	10	20	30	40	50	60	70	80	90	100	110	120
Miles	6.2	12.4	18.6	24.9	31	37.3	43.5	49.7	56	62	68.3	74.6

Tyre pressures

lb/sq in	15	18	20	22	24	26	28	30	33	35
kg/sq cm	1.1	1.3	1.4	1.5	1.7	1.8	2	2.1	2.3	2.5

Liquids

gallons	1.1	2.2	3.3	4.4	5.5	pints	0.44	0.88	1.76
litres	5	10	15	20	25	litres	0.25	0.5	1

I have nothing to declare Não tenho nada a declarar
nowng ten-yoo nah-duh uh duh-klarar

I have the usual allowances of alcohol/tobacco Trago as
quantidades de álcool/tabaco autorizadas
*trah-goo ush kwantee-dah-dush dalkoo-ol/toobah-koo
owtooree-zah-dush*

I have two bottles of wine to declare Tenho duas garrafas de
vinho a declarar
ten-yoo doo-ush garrah-fush duh veen-yoo uh duh-klarar

My wife/husband and I have a joint passport A minha
mulher/o meu marido e eu temos um passaporte familiar
*uh meen-yuh mool-yehr/oo may-oo mareedoo ee ay-oo tay-
mooz oom passuh-port fameel-yar*

The children are on this passport As crianças estão neste
passaporte
ush kree-ansush shtowng naysht passuh-port

I am a British national Eu sou de nacionalidade britânica
ay-oo soh duh nas-yoonalee-dahd bree-tahnikuh

We are here on holiday Estamos aqui de férias
shtah-mooz akee duh fehr-yush

I am here on business Estou aqui em viagem de negócios
shtoh akee ayng vee-ah-jayng duh negoss-yoosh

I have an entry visa Tenho um visto de entrada
ten-yoo oom veeshtoo dayn-trah-duh

See also NUMBERS

What is the date today? A quantos estamos hoje?
    *uh **kwantoosh shtah**-mooz ohj*

It's the ...   Hoje é dia ... *ohj e dee-uh ...*

1st of March	**2nd of June**
1 de Março	2 de Junho
*preemay-roo duh **marsoo***	*doysh duh **joon**-yoo*

We will arrive on the 29th of August
Chegamos no dia vinte e nove de Agosto
*shuh**gah**-moosh noo **dee**-uh veent ee nov da**gosht**oo*

1984 mil novecentos e oitenta e quatro
*meel nov-**sentooz** ee **oy**tent ee **kwa**troo*

Monday	segunda-feira	*segoonduh-**fay**-ruh*
Tuesday	terça-feira	*tehr-suh-**fay**-ruh*
Wednesday	quarta-feira	*kwartuh-**fay**-ruh*
Thursday	quinta-feira	*keentuh-**fay**-ruh*
Friday	sexta-feira	*seshtuh-**fay**-ruh*
Saturday	sábado	*sabadoo*
Sunday	domingo	*doomeengoo*

January	**May**	**September**
Janeiro	Maio	Setembro
janay-roo	*my-oo*	*setembroo*
February	**June**	**October**
Fevereiro	Junho	Outubro
*fuv-**ray**-roo*	*joon-yoo*	*oh-**toob**roo*
March	**July**	**November**
Março	Julho	Novembro
marsoo	*jool-yoo*	*noovembroo*
April	**August**	**December**
Abril	Agosto	Dezembro
abreel	*agoshtoo*	*dezembroo*

You will be asked to pay for treatment on the spot, so medical insurance is essential. It is much better to go to a private dentist than to go to hospital.

I need to see the dentist (urgently) Preciso de ir ao dentista (urgentemente)
*pre-**see**zoo deer ow den-**teesh**tuh (oorjent-**ment**)*

I have toothache Doem-me os dentes
do-aying-muh oosh dentsh

I've broken a tooth Tenho um dente partido
*ten-yoo oom dent par-**tee**doo*

A filling has come out Caíu-me um chumbo
*kayoo-muh oom **shoom**boo*

My gums are bleeding/are sore As minhas gengivas estão a sangrar/Doem-me as gengivas
*ush **meen**-yush jen-**jee**vush shtowng uh san**grar**/**do**-aying-muh ush jen-**jee**vush*

Please give me an injection Por favor, dê-me uma injecção
*poor fa**vor** day-muh **oom**uh eenje-**sowng***

My dentures need repairing A minha placa tem que ser arranjada
*uh **meen**-yuh **plah**-kuh tayng kuh sehr arran**jah**-duh*

THE DENTIST MAY SAY:

Tenho que lho tirar
*ten-yoo kuh l-yoo tee**rar***
I shall have to take it out

Precisa de um chumbo
*pre-**see**zuh doom **shoom**boo*
You need a filling

Talvez lhe doa um pouco
*tal**vesh** l-yuh **doh**-uh oom **poh**-koo*
This might hurt a bit

bad
mau
mow

beautiful
lindo
leendoo

bitter
amargo
amargoo

clean
limpo
leempoo

cold
frio
free-oo

difficult
difícil
deefee-seel

dirty
sujo
soojoo

easy
fácil
fah-seel

excellent
excelente
eesh-suh-lent

far
longe
lonj

fast
rápido
rapidoo

flat
plano
plah-noo

good
bom
bong

hard
duro
dooroo

heavy
pesado
puh-zah-doo

horrible
horrivel
oh-reevel

hot
quente
kent

interesting
interessante
eentuh-re-sant

light
leve
lev

long
longo
longoo

lovely
maravilhoso
maruh-veel-yoh-zoo

near
perto
pehrtoo

new
novo
noh-voo

old
velho
vel-yoo

pleasant
agradável
agruh-dah-vel

rough
áspero
ashperoo

short
curto
koortoo

slow
lento
lentoo

smooth
macio
masee-oo

soft
suave
swahv

sour
ácido
assidoo

spicy
picante
peekant

strong
forte
fort

sweet
doce
dohss

unpleasant
desagradável
duz-agruh-dah-vel

warm
tépido
tepidoo

weak
fraco
frah-koo

Where is the nearest post office? Onde
fica a estação dos correios mais próxima?
*onduh feekuh uh shta-sowng doosh koo-
rayoosh mysh prossimuh*

How do I get to the airport? Como se
vai para o aeroporto?
koh-moo suh vy pro uh-ehroo-portoo

Is this the right way to the cathedral?
É este o caminho para a catedral?
e aysht oo kameen-yoo pra katuh-dral

**I am looking for the tourist
information office** Procuro o turismo
prookooroo oo tooreej-moo

Is it far to walk/by car? Fica muito
longe para ir a pé/de carro?
*feekuh mweentoo lonj paruh eer uh
pe/duh karroo*

Which road do I take for ...? Qual a
estrada que vai para ...?
kwal uh shtrah-duh kuh vy paruh ...

Is this the turning for ...? É aqui que se
vira para ...?
e akee kuh suh veeruh paruh ...

How do I get on to the motorway?
Como se vai para a autoestrada?
koh-moo suh vy pra owtoo-shtrah-duh

I have lost my way Perdi-me
perdee-muh

Can you show me on the map? Pode
mostrar-me no mapa?
pod mooshtrar-muh noo mah-puh

How long will it take to get there?
Quanto tempo demora a chegar lá?
*kwantoo tempoo duh-moruh uh shuh-gar
la*

corner	a esquina
	shkeenuh
left	a esquerda
	shkehr-duh
near	perto de
	pehrtoo duh
over	por cima de
	poor seemuh duh
over there	além
	alayng
right	a direita
	deeray-tuh
road sign	o sinal de trânsito
	seenal duh tranzeetoo
station	a estação
	shta-sowng
straight on	sempre em frente
	sempruh ayng frent
through	por
	poor
under	por baixo de
	poor by-shoo duh

See also BODY
If you visit the doctor you will have to pay on the spot, so
medical insurance is essential. If it is not something urgent, it's
better to see a private doctor rather than go to the hospital.

I need a doctor Preciso de ir ao médico
pre-seezoo deer ow medikoo

**Can I have an appointment with the
doctor?** Posso ter uma consulta com o
médico?
*possoo tehr oomuh konsooltuh kong oo
medikoo*

My son/wife is ill O meu filho/a minha
mulher está doente
*oo may-oo feel-yoo/uh meen-yuh mool-
yehr shta doo-ent*

I have a sore throat/a stomach upset
Dói-me a garganta/o estômago
doy-muh uh gargantuh/oo shtoh-magoo

He has diarrhoea/earache Ele tem
diarreia/dores de ouvidos
*ayl tayng dee-uh-rayuh/dorush doh-
veedoosh*

I am constipated Tenho prisão de ventre
ten-yoo preezowng duh ventruh

I have a pain here/in my chest Dói-me
aqui/o peito
doy-muh akee/oo paytoo

She has a temperature Ela tem febre
eluh tayng februh

He has been stung/bitten Ele foi
picado/mordido
ayl foy peekah-doo/moordeedoo

He can't breathe/walk Ele não pode
respirar/andar
ayl nowng pod rushpeerar/andar

cough
a tosse
tohss

cut
o corte
kort

faint, to
desmaiar
dush-my-ar

food poisoning
a intoxicação
alimentar
*eentoxee-ka-
sowng alee-
mentar*

hay fever
a febre dos fenos
*februh doosh fay-
noosh*

headache
a dor de cabeça
dor duh kabay-suh

I feel dizzy Sinto-me tonto
seentoo-muh tontoo

I can't sleep/swallow Não posso
dormir/engolir
nowng possoo doormeer/ayngoo-leer

She has been sick Ela vomitou
eluh voomeetoh

I am a diabetic/pregnant Sou
diabético/Estou grávida
soh dee-uh-betikoo/shtoh graviduh

I am allergic to penicillin/cortisone
Sou alérgico à penicilina/cortisona
*soh alehr-jikoo a punneesee-leenuh/
koortee-zonuh*

I have high blood pressure Tenho a
tensão alta
ten-yoo uh tayn-sowng altuh

**My blood group is A positive/O
negative** O meu grupo sanguíneo é A
positivo/O negativo
*oo may-oo groopoo sangeen-yoo e a
poozee-teevoo/o nuh-guh-teevoo*

THE DOCTOR MAY SAY:

Tem que ficar na cama
tayng kuh feekar nuh kah-muh
You must stay in bed

Ele tem que ir para o hospital
ayl tayng kuh eer pro oshpeetal
He will have to go to hospital

Tem que ser operado
tayng kuh sehr oh-perah-doo
You will need an operation

Tome isto três/quatro vezes por dia
*tom eeshtoo traysh/kwatroo vay-zush poor
dee-uh*
Take this three/four times a day

---

inflamed
inflamado
eemfla-mah-doo

injection
a injecção
een-je-sowng

medicine
o remédio
ruh-med-yoo

painful
doloroso
dooloo-roh-zoo

pill
o comprimido
kompree-meedoo

poisoning
o envenenamento
aym-vuh-nennuh-mentoo

tablet
o comprimido
kompree-meedoo

unconscious
inconsciente
eenkonsh-see-ent

See also WINES AND SPIRITS

A black/white coffee, please Um
café/um café com leite, por favor
*oom kuh-fe/oom kuh-fe kong layt poor
favor*

Two cups of tea Duas chávenas de chá
doo-ush sha-venush duh sha

A pot of tea Um chá
oom sha

A glass of lemonade Uma limonada
oomuh leemoonah-duh

A bottle of mineral water Uma garrafa
de água mineral
oomuh garrah-fuh dahg-wuh meenuh-ral

Do you have ...? Tem ...?
tayng ...

With ice, please Com gelo, por favor
kong jayloo poor favor

Another coffee, please Outro café, por
favor
oh-troo kuh-fe poor favor

beer
a cerveja
servay-juh

coke
a coca cola
kokuh-koluh

**drinking
chocolate**
o chocolate
shookoo-lat

drinking water
a água
ahg-wuh

fruit juice
o sumo de frutas
*soomoo duh
frootush*

lemon tea
o carioca de limão
*karee-okuh duh
leemowng*

milk
o leite
layt

shandy
a cerveja e
limonada
*servay-juh ee
leemoo-nah-duh*

soft drink
a bebida leve
buh-beeduh lev

with milk
com leite
kong layt

See also ACCIDENTS – CARS, BREAKDOWNS, CAR PARTS, PETROL
STATION, POLICE, ROAD SIGNS
Speed limits are 60 km/h in urban areas, 90 km/h on ordinary
roads and 120 km/h on motorways.

What is the speed limit on this road?
Qual é o limite de velocidade nesta
estrada?
*kwal e oo leemeet duh veloo-seedahd
neshtuh shtrah-duh*

Are seat belts compulsory? Os cintos de
segurança são obrigatórios?
*oosh seentoosh duh segoo-ransuh sowng
oh-breeguh-tor-yoosh*

Is there a toll on this motorway? Há
portagem nesta autoestrada?
*a poortah-jayng neshtuh owtoo-shtrah-
duh*

What is causing this hold-up? Qual é a
causa deste engarrafamento?
*kwal e uh kowzuh daysht ayngarrah-fuh-
mentoo*

Is there a short-cut? Há um atalho?
a oom atal-yoo

Where can I park? Onde posso
estacionar?
onduh possoo shtass-yoonar

Is there a car park nearby? Há um
parque de estacionamento perto?
*a oom park duh shtass-yoonuh-mentoo
pehrtoo*

Can I park here? Posso estacionar aqui?
possoo shtass-yoonar akee

How long can I stay here? Quanto
tempo posso ficar aqui?
kwantoo tempoo possoo feekar akee

Do I need a parking disc? Preciso de um
disco de estacionamento?
*pre-seezoo doom deeshkoo duh shtass-
yoonuh-mentoo*

driving licence
a carta de
condução
*kartuh duh
kondoo-sowng*

green card
a carta verde
kartuh vehrd

major road
a estrada principal
*shtrah-duh
preensee-pal*

minor road
a estrada
secundária
*shtrah-duh suh-
koon-dar-yuh*

one-way
o sentido único
senteedoo oonikoo

parking meter
o parquímetro
parkee-metroo

parking ticket
a multa
mooltuh

sign
o sinal de trânsito
*seenal duh
tranzeetoo*

traffic lights
os semáforos
suh-mafooroosh

See also DRINKS, FOOD, ORDERING, PAYING
There are 4 grades of Portuguese restaurants: luxury, 1st class, 2nd class and 3rd class indicated by a star system. Tourist menus are good value.

Is there a restaurant/café near here?
Há um restaurante/um café perto?
*a oom rushtoh-**rant**/oom kuh-**fe pehr**too*

A table for four please Uma mesa para quatro, por favor
*oomuh may-zuh paruh **kwat**roo poor favor*

May we see the menu? Pode-nos dar a ementa?
*pod-noosh dar uh ee** mentuh***

We'll take the set menu please
Queremos a refeição da casa, por favor
*kray-mooz uh ruh-fay-**sowng** duh **kah**-zuh poor favor*

We'd like a drink first Queremos uma bebida primeiro
*kray-mooz **oomuh** bebeeduh pree-**may**roo*

Could we have some more bread/water? Pode trazer mais pão/água?
*pod trazehr mysh powng/**ahg**-wuh*

We'd like a dessert/some mineral water Queremos a sobremesa/água mineral
*kray-mooz uh sobruh-**mayzuh**/**ahg**-wuh meenuh-**ral***

The bill, please A conta, por favor
*uh **kon**tuh poor favor*

Is service included? O serviço está incluído?
*oo ser**vees**soo shta een-**klwee**doo*

cheese
o queijo
kay-joo

main course
o prato principal
prah-too preensee-pal

sandwich
a sanduíche
*sand-**weesh***

soup
a sopa
sopuh

starter
a entrada
*ayn-**trah**-duh*

terrace
a esplanada
shplanah-duh

vegetables
os legumes
*luh-**goom**ush*

See also ACCIDENTS, BREAKDOWNS, DENTIST, DOCTOR

There's a fire! Há fogo!
a foh-goo

Call a doctor/an ambulance! Chamem
um médico/uma ambulância!
*shah-mayng oom medikoo/oomuh
amboolanss-yuh*

We must get him to hospital Temos
que o levar ao hospital
tay-moosh kee oo levar ow oshpeetal

Fetch help quickly Procure ajuda
depressa
prookoor ajooduh depressuh

He can't swim Ele não sabe nadar
ayl nowng sahb nadar

Get the police Chame a polícia
shahm uh pooleess-yuh

Where's the nearest hospital? Onde fica
o hospital mais próximo?
*onduh feekuh oo oshpeetal mysh pro-
seemoo*

I've lost my credit card/wallet Perdi o
meu cartão de crédito/a minha carteira
*perdee oo may-oo kartowng duh
kreditoo/uh meen-yuh kartay-ruh*

My child is missing Não encontro o meu
filho
nowng ayng-kontroo oo may-oo feel-yoo

My passport has been stolen O meu
passaporte foi roubado
oo may-oo passuh-port foy roh-bah-doo

I've forgotten my ticket/my key
Esqueci-me do meu bilhete/da minha
chave
*shke-see-muh doo may-oo beel-yet/duh
meen-yuh shahv*

coastguard
a polícia marítima
*pooleess-yuh ma-
reetimuh*

consulate
o consulado
konsoo-lah-doo

embassy
a embaixada
aym-by-shah-duh

fire brigade
os bombeiros
bombay-roosh

fire!
fogo!
foh-goo

help!
socorro!
sookorroo

**lost property
office**
a secção de
perdidos e achados
*seksowng duh
perdeedooz ee
ashah-doosh*

police!
polícia!
pooleess-yuh

stop thief!
agarra que é
ladrão!
*agaruh kee e
ladrowng*

See also NIGHTLIFE, SIGHTSEEING

Are there any local festivals? Há
algumas festas locais?
a algoomush feshtush lookysh

**Can you recommend something for
the children?** Pode recomendar alguma
coisa para as crianças?
*pod rekoomen-dar algoomuh koyzuh prash
kree-ansush*

What is there to do in the evenings? O
que é que há para fazer à noite?
oo kee e kee a paruh fazehr a noyt

Where is there a cinema/theatre? Onde
é que há um cinema/um teatro?
*ondee e kee a oom seenay-muh/oom tee-
ah-troo*

Where can we go to a concert? Onde é
que há um concerto?
ondee e kee a oom konsehr-too

Can you book the tickets for us? Pode
marcar-nos os bilhetes?
pod markar-nooz ooj beel-yetsh

Are there any night clubs/discos? Há
algumas boites/discotecas?
a algoomush bwatsh/deeshkoo-tekush

Is there a swimming pool? Há piscina?
a peesh-seenuh

Can we go fishing/riding? Podemos
pescar/andar a cavalo?
*pooday-moosh pushkar/andar uh kavah-
loo*

Where can we play tennis/golf? Onde
podemos jogar ténis/golfe?
*onduh pooday-moosh joogar
tayneesh/golf*

admission charge	o bilhete de entrada *beel-yet daynt-trah-duh*
bar	o bar *bar*
booking office	a bilheteira *beel-yuh-tay-ruh*
club	o clube *kloob*
fun fair	a feira *fay-ruh*
jazz	o jazz *jazz*
orchestra	a orquestra *or-keshtruh*
play	a peça *pessuh*
show	o espectáculo *shpe-takooloo*
ticket	o bilhete *beel-yet*

What time is the next sailing? A que horas parte o próximo barco?
uh kee orush part oo prossimoo barkoo

A return ticket for one car, two adults and two children Um bilhete de ida e volta para um carro, dois adultos e duas crianças
oom beel-yet duh eeduh ee voltuh paruh oom karroo doyz adooltooz ee doo-ush kree-ansush

How long does the crossing take? Quanto tempo demora a travessia?
kwantoo tempoo demoruh uh travuh-see-uh

Are there any cabins/reclining seats? Há camarotes/bancos reclináveis?
a kamuh-rotsh/bankoosh ruh-kleenah-vaysh

Is there a bar/TV lounge? Há um bar/uma sala de televisão?
a oom bar/oomuh sah-luh duh tuh-luh-veezowng

Where are the toilets? Onde fica a casa de banho?
onduh feekuh uh kah-zuh duh bahn-yoo

Where is the duty-free shop? Onde fica a loja franca?
onduh feekuh uh lojuh frankuh

Can we go out on deck? Podemos ir para o convés?
pooday-mooz eer pro komvesh

What is the sea like today? Como está o mar hoje?
koh-moo shta oo mar ohj

---

captain
o capitão
kapee-towng

crew
a tripulação
treepoo-la-sowng

hovercraft
o hovercraft
hovercraft

life jacket
o colete de salvação
koolet duh salvuh-sowng

lifeboat
o salva-vidas
salvuh-veedush

purser
o comissário de bordo
koomeesar-yoo duh bordoo

rough
bravo
brah-voo

ship
o barco
barkoo

smooth
calmo
kalmoo

the Channel
o Canal da Mancha
kanal duh manshuh

beef
a carne de vaca
*karn duh **vah**-kuh*

bread
o pão
powng

butter
a manteiga
*man**tay**-guh*

cheese
o queijo
***kay**-joo*

chicken
a galinha
*ga**leen**-yuh*

coffee
o café
*kuh-**fe***

cream
a nata
***nah**-tuh*

eggs
os ovos
ovoosh

fish
o peixe
paysh

flour
a farinha
*fa**reen**-yuh*

ham
o presunto
*pruh-**zoon**too*

jam
o doce
dohss

kidneys
os rins
reensh

kilo
o quilo
keeloo

lamb
a carne de borrego
*karn duh boo**ray**-goo*

litre
o litro
leetroo

liver
o fígado
***fee**gadoo*

margarine
a margarina
*marguh-**reen**uh*

milk
o leite
layt

mince
a carne picada
*karn pee**kah**-duh*

mustard
a mostarda
*moosh-**tarduh***

oil
o óleo
***ol**-yoo*

pepper
a pimenta
*pee**men**tuh*

pork
a carne de porco
*karn duh **porkoo***

pound
o meio-quilo
*mayoo-**keeloo***

rice
o arroz
*a**rosh***

salt
o sal
sal

soup
a sopa
sopuh

steak
o bife
beef

sugar
o açúcar
*a**sookar***

tea
o chá
sha

tin
a lata
***lah**-tuh*

veal
a carne de vitela
*karn duh vee**teluh***

vinegar
o vinagre
*vee**nah**-gruh*

yoghurt
o iogurte
*yo**goort***

apples
as maçãs
ma-**sansh**

asparagus
os espargos
shpar**goosh**

aubergine
a beringela
beren-**jeluh**

avocado
o abacate
abuh-**kat**

bananas
as bananas
banah-**nush**

beetroot
a beterraba
betuh-**rah**-buh

carrots
as cenouras
suh-**noh**-rush

cauliflower
a couve-flor
kohv-**flor**

celery
o aipo
y-**poo**

cherries
as cerejas
suh-**ray**-jush

courgettes
as courgettes
koor**jetsh**

cucumber
o pepino
puh-**peenoo**

french beans
o feijão verde
fay-**jowng** vehrd

garlic
o alho
al-**yoo**

grapefruit
a toranja
tooran-**juh**

grapes
as uvas
oovush

leeks
os alhos franceses
al-yoosh fransay-
zush

lemon
o limão
lee**mowng**

lettuce
a alface
al**fass**

melon
o melão
muh-**lowng**

mushrooms
os cogumelos
koogoo-**meloosh**

olives
as azeitonas
azay-**tonush**

onions
as cebolas
suh-**bolush**

oranges
as laranjas
laran-jush

peaches
os pêssegos
pay-suh-goosh

pears
as peras
pehrush

peas
as ervilhas
ehr-**veel**-yush

pepper
o pimento
pee**mentoo**

pineapple
o ananás
anuh-**nash**

plums
as ameixas
amay-**shush**

potatoes
as batatas
batah-**tush**

radishes
os rabanetes
rabuh-**netsh**

raspberries
as framboesas
fram-**bway**-zush

spinach
os espinafres
shpeenaf-**rush**

strawberries
os morangos
moor**angoosh**

tomatoes
os tomates
too**matsh**

Where can we buy souvenirs of the cathedral? Onde é que podemos comprar lembranças desta catedral?
ondee e kuh pooday-moosh komprar laym-bransush deshtuh katuh-dral

Where is the nearest gift shop? Onde fica a loja de lembranças mais próxima?
onduh feekuh uh lojuh duh laym-bransush mysh prossimuh

I want to buy a present for my husband/wife Quero comprar um presente para o meu marido/a minha mulher
kehroo komprar oom prezent pro may-oo mareedoo/uh meen-yuh mool-yehr

What is the local/regional speciality? Qual é a especialidade local/regional?
kwal e uh shpuss-yalee-dahd lookal/ruj-yoonal

Is this hand-made? Isto é feito à mão?
eeshtoo e faytoo a mowng

Have you anything suitable for a young child? Tem alguma coisa para crianças?
tayng algoomuh koy-zuh paruh kree-ansush

I want something cheaper/more expensive Quero uma coisa mais barata/mais cara
kehroo oomuh koy-zuh mysh barah-tuh/mysh kah-ruh

Will this cheese/wine travel well? Este queijo/este vinho aguenta bem a viagem?
aysht kay-joo/aysht veen-yoo agwentuh bayng uh vee-ah-jayng

Please wrap it up for me Por favor, embrulhe-me isso
poor favor aymbrool-yuh-muh eesoo

bracelet a bracelete *brassuh-let*	
brooch o broche *brosh*	
chocolates os chocolates *shookoo-latsh*	
earrings os brincos *breenkoosh*	
flowers as flores *florush*	
necklace o colar *koolar*	
ornament o bibelot *beebuh-loh*	
perfume o perfume *perfoom*	
pottery a cerâmica *suh-rahmikuh*	
ring o anel *anel*	
watch o relógio *ruh-loj-yoo*	

Nouns

Portuguese nouns are *masculine* or *feminine*, and their gender is shown by the words for 'the' and 'a' used before them (the 'article'):

MASCULINE	FEMININE
o/um castelo *the/a castle*	**a/uma** mesa *the/a table*
os castelos/(**uns**) castelos	**as** mesa/(**umas**) mesas
the castles/castles	*the tables/tables*

It is usually possible to tell whether a noun is masculine or feminine by its ending: nouns ending in **-o** or **-or** are usually masculine, while those ending in **-a**, **-agem**, **-dade** and **-tude** tend to be feminine. There are exceptions, however, and it's best to learn the noun and the article together.

Plural

Nouns ending in a vowel form the plural by adding **-s**, while those ending in a consonant usually add **-es**. The exception to this is words ending in an **-m** which change to **-ns** in the plural and words ending in **-l** which change to **-is** in the plural: *hotel-hotéis*.

NOTE: When used after the words **a** (to), **de** (of), **em** (in) and **por** (by), the articles (and many other words) contract:

a + **as** → **às** *ash*	to the
de + **um** → **dum** *doom*	of a
em + **uma** → **numa** *noomuh*	to a
por + **os** → **pelos** *peloosh*	by the

'This', 'That', 'These', 'Those'

These depend on the gender and number of the noun they represent:

este menino	*this boy*	**esta** menina	*this girl*
estes meninos	*these boys*	**estas** meninas	*these girls*
esse menino	*that boy*	**essa** menina	*that girl*
esses meninos	*those boys*	**essas** meninas	*those girls*
aquele menino	*that boy (over there)*	**aquela** menina	*that girl (over there)*
aqueles meninos	*those boys (over there)*	**aquelas** meninas	*those girls (over there)*

Adjectives

Adjectives normally follow the noun they describe in Portuguese, e.g. a maçã verde (the green apple). Some common exceptions which precede the noun are:

muito much, many; **pouco** few; **tanto** so much, so many; **primeiro** first; **último** last; **bom** good; **mau** bad; **nenhum** no, not any; **grande** great.

Portuguese adjectives have to reflect the gender of the noun they describe. To make an adjective *feminine*, -o endings change to -a, and -or and -ês change to -ora and -esa. Otherwise they generally have the same form for both genders. Thus:

MASCULINE	o livro **vermelho**	FEMININE	a saia **vermelha**
	(the red book)		(the red skirt)
	o homem **falador**		a mulher **faladora**
	(the talkative man)		(the talkative woman)

To make an adjective plural follow the general rules given for nouns.

'My', 'Your', 'His', 'Her'

These words also depend on the gender and number of the following noun and not on the sex of the 'owner'.

	with masculine	with feminine	with plural nouns
my	o **meu**	a **minha**	os **meus**/as **minhas**
	mayoo	*meen-yuh*	*mayoosh/meen-yush*
his/her/			
its/your	o **seu** *sayoo*	a **sua** *soo-uh*	os **seus**/as **suas**
our	o **nosso** *nossoo*	a **nossa** *nossuh*	os **nossos**/as **nossas**
their/your	o **seu** *sayoo*	a **sua** *soo-uh*	os **seus**/as **suas**

NOTE: Since **o seu**, **a sua**, etc can mean 'his', 'her', 'your', etc, Portuguese will often replace them with the words for 'of him', 'of her', 'of you', etc (**dele, dela, de você**, etc) in order to avoid confusion.

os livros **dela**	her books
os livros **de você**	your books
os livros **deles**	their books

Pronouns

SUBJECT		OBJECT	
I	**eu** *ay-oo*	me	**me** *muh*
you	**você** *voh-se*	you	**o/a** *oo/uh*
he	**ele** *ayl*	him	**o** *oo*
she	**ela** *eluh*	her	**a** *uh*
it	**ele/ela** *ayl/eluh*	it	**o/a** *oo/uh*
we	**nós** *nosh*	us	**nos** *noosh*
you	**vocês** *voh-sesh*	you	**os/as** *oosh/ush*
they	(*masc*) **eles** *aylush*	them	(*masc*) **os** *oosh*
	(*fem*) **elas** *elush*		(*fem*) **as** *ush*

NOTES

1. Subject pronouns are normally not used except for emphasis or to avoid confusion:

> **eu** vou para Lisboa e **ele** vai para Coimbra
> I'm going to Lisbon and he's going to Coimbra

2. Object pronouns are usually placed after the verb and joined with a hyphen: vejo-**o** I see him

However in sentences beginning with a 'question word' or a 'negative word' the pronoun goes in front of the verb:

> quando **o** viu?   when did you see him?
> não **o** vi   I did not see him

Also in sentences beginning with 'that' and 'who', etc ('subordinate clauses') the pronoun precedes the verb:

> sei que **o** viu   I know that you saw him
> o homem que **o** viu   the man who saw him

3. **Me** also = to me and **nos** = to us, but **lhe** = to him/to her/to it/to you and **lhes** = to them/to you.

4. When two pronouns are used together they are often shortened. The verb will also change spelling if it ends in **-r**, **-s**, **-z** or a nasal sound:

dá-mo	(= **dá** + **me** + **o**)	he gives me it
dê-lho	(= **dê** + **lhe** + **o**)	give him it
fá-lo	(= **faz** + **o**)	he does it
dão-nos	(= **dão** + **os** or	they give them
	dão + **nos**)	*or* they give us

5. The pronoun following a preposition has the same form as the subject pronoun, except for **mim** (me), and **si** (you).

Verbs

There are 3 main patterns of endings for verbs in Portuguese - those ending in **-ar**, **-er** and **-ir** in the dictionary.

cantar to sing	**comer** to eat	**partir** to leave
canto I sing	**como** I eat	**parto** I leave
canta he/she/it sings/you sing	**come** he/she/it eats/you eat	**parte** he/she/it leaves/you leave
cantamos we sing	**comemos** we eat	**partimos** we leave
cantam they/you sing	**comem** they/you eat	**partem** they/you leave

And in the past tense:

cantei I sang	**comi** I ate	**parti** I left
cantou he/she/it/ you sang	**comeu** he/she/it/ you ate	**partiu** he/she/it/ you left
cantámos we sang	**comemos** we ate	**partimos** we left
cantaram they/you sang	**comeram** they/you ate	**partiram** they/you left

Four of the most common verbs are irregular:

ser to be	**estar** to be
sou I am	**estou** I am
é he/she/it is/ you are	**está** he/she/it is/ you are
somos we are	**estamos** we are
são they/you are	**estão** they/you are
ter to have	**ir** to go
tenho I have	**vou** I go
tem he/she/it has/ you have	**vai** he/she/it goes/ you go
temos we have	**vamos** we go
têm they/you have	**vão** they/you go

Portuguese has two forms of address, formal and informal. If you know someone very well you say *tu*. The formal greeting is *o senhor* for gentlemen and *a senhora* for ladies. In Portugal you shake hands on meeting and on saying goodbye.

Hello Olá
oh-la

Good morning/good afternoon/good evening Bom dia/boa tarde/boa noite
bong dee-uh/boh-uh tard/boh-uh noyt

Goodbye Adeus
aday-oosh

Good night Boa noite
boh-uh noyt

How do you do? Como está?
koh-moo shta

Pleased to meet you Prazer em conhecê-lo
prazehr ayng koon-yuh-seh-loo

How nice to see you Prazer em vê-lo
prazehr ayng veh-loo

How are you? Como está?
koh-moo shta

Fine thank you Bem obrigado
bayng oh-breegah-doo

See you soon Até breve
ate brev

See you later Até logo
ate logoo

I'd like to make an appointment
Queria marcar a vez
kree-uh markar uh vesh

A cut and blow-dry, please Cortar e
secar, por favor
koortar ee sekar poor favor

A shampoo and set Lavar e fazer mise
lavar ee fazehr meez

Not too short Não muito curto
nowng mweentoo koortoo

I'd like it layered Queria o cabelo cortado
em dégradé
*kree-uh oo kabay-loo koortah-doo ayng
day-graday*

Not too much off the back/the fringe
Não corte muito atrás/a franja
nowng kort mweentoo atrash/uh franjuh

Take more off the top/sides Corte mais
por cima/dos lados
kort mysh poor seemuh/doosh lah-doosh

My hair is permed/tinted Tenho uma
permanente/o cabelo pintado
*ten-yoo oomuh permuh-nent/oo kabay-
loo peentah-doo*

My hair is naturally curly/straight O
meu cabelo é encaracolado/liso
*oo may-oo kabay-loo e ayng-karuh-
koolah-doo/leezoo*

It is too hot Está quente demais
shta kent duh-mysh

I'd like a conditioner/some hair spray
Queria um acondicionador/laca
*kree-uh oom akondeess-yoonuh-dor/lah-
kuh*

gown
o penteador
pentee-uh-dor

haircut
o corte de cabelo
kort duh kabay-loo

long
comprido
kompreedoo

parting
a risca
reeshkuh

perm
a permanente
permanent

shampoo
o shampô
shampoh

short
curto
koortoo

streaks
as madeixas
maday-shush

styling mousse
a mousse
mooss

towel
a toalha
too-al-yuh

trim, to
aparar
aparar

See also ACCOMMODATION, ROOM SERVICE, PAYING

**I have reserved a room in the name
of ...** Reservei um quarto em nome de ...
*ruh-zervay oom **kwar**too ayng nom duh ...*

**I confirmed my booking by phone/by
letter** Confirmei a minha reserva pelo
telefone/por carta
*komfeer**may** uh **meen**-yuh ruh-**zehr**vuh
ploo tuh-luh-**fon**/poor **kar**tuh*

Could you have my luggage taken up?
Podem levar a minha bagagem para o
quarto?
*po**day**ng le**var** uh **meen**-yuh ba**gah**-jayng
pro **kwar**too*

What time is breakfast/dinner? A que
horas é o pequeno almoço/o jantar?
*uh kee **or**uz e oo puh-**kay**-noo al**moh**-
soo/oo jan**tar***

Can we have breakfast in our room?
Podemos tomar o pequeno almoço no
quarto?
*poo**day**-moosh too**mar** oo puh-**kay**-noo
al**moh**-soo noo **kwar**too*

Please call me at seven thirty Por
favor, acorde-me às sete e meia
*poor fa**vor** a**kord**-muh ash set e **may**uh*

Can I have my key? Pode-me dar a
chave?
pod**-muh dar uh **shahv

We'll be back very late Regressamos
muito tarde
*rugruh-**sah**-moosh **mween**too tard*

I want to stay an extra night Quero
ficar mais uma noite
***keh**roo fee**kar** myz **oom**uh noyt*

I shall be leaving tomorrow morning
Parto amanhã de manhã
par**too aman-**yang** duh man**yang

bar o bar	*bar*
desk a recepção	*ruh-**sep**sowng*
lift o elevador	*eeluh-vuh-**dor***
lounge a sala de estar	***sah**-luh dush**tar***
manager o gerente	*juh-**rent***
porter o porteiro	*poor**tay**-roo*
reservation a reserva	*ruh-**zehr**vuh*
restaurant o restaurante	*rushtoh-**rant***
room service o serviço de quarto	*ser**vee**soo duh **kwar**too*
stay a estadia	*shta**dee**-uh*
TV lounge a sala de televisão	***sah**-luh duh tuh-luh-vee**zowng***

Where do I check in my luggage? Onde
faço o check-in?
onduh fah-soo oo check-in

**Where is the luggage from the Lisbon
flight/train?** Onde está a bagagem do
voo/do comboio de Lisboa?
*onduh shta uh bagah-jayng doo voh-
oo/doo komboyoo duh leej-boh-uh*

Our luggage has not arrived A nossa
bagagem não chegou
uh nossuh bagah-jayng nowng shuh-goh

My suitcase was damaged in transit A
minha mala estragou-se na viagem
*uh meen-yuh mah-luh shtragoh-suh nuh
vee-ah-jayng*

Where is the left-luggage office? Onde
fica o depósito de bagagem?
*onduh feekuh oo duh-pozitoo duh bagah-
jayng*

Are there any luggage trolleys? Há
carrinhos para as bagagens?
a kareen-yoosh prash bagah-jaynsh

It's very heavy É muito pesada
e mweentoo puh-zah-duh

Can you help me with my bags? Pode
ajudar-me a levar os meus sacos?
*pod ajoodar-muh uh luh-var ooj may-oosh
sah-koosh*

Take my bag to a taxi Leve o meu saco
para um táxi
lev oo may-oo sah-koo proom taxee

I can manage this one myself Eu levo
este
ay-oo levoo aysht

I sent my luggage on in advance
Despachei a minha bagagem antes
*dush-pashay uh meen-yuh bagah-jayng
antsh*

baggage reclaim
o tapete rolante
tapet roolant

excess luggage
o excesso de
bagagem
*eesh-sessoo duh
bagah-jayng*

flight bag
o saco de viagem
*sah-koo duh vee-
ah-jayng*

hand luggage
a bagagem de mão
*bagah-jayng duh
mowng*

locker
o armário para a
bagagem
*armar-yoo pra
bagah-jayng*

**luggage
allowance**
o limite de peso
autorizado
*leemeet duh pay-
zoo owtooree-zah-
doo*

luggage rack
a rede
red

porter
o carregador
karruh-guh-dor

trunk
a mala
mah-luh

See also DIRECTIONS

Where can I buy a local map? Onde posso comprar um mapa
local?
*onduh **possoo** komprar oom **mah**-puh loo**kal***

Have you got a town plan? Tem um mapa da cidade?
*tayng oom **mah**-puh duh see**dahd***

I want a street map of the city Quero um mapa com as ruas
da cidade
keh**roo oom **mah**-puh kong ush **roo**-ush duh see**dahd

I need a road map of ... Preciso de um mapa das estradas de ...
*pre-**see**zoo doom **mah**-puh dush **shtrah**-dush duh ...*

Can I get a map at the tourist office? Posso arranjar um
mapa no turismo?
***possoo** arranjar oom **mah**-puh noo too**reej**-moo*

Can you show me on the map? Pode-me mostrar no mapa?
*pod-muh moosh**trar** noo **mah**-puh*

Do you have a guidebook in English? Tem um guia
turístico em inglês?
*tayng oom **ghee**-uh too**reesh**-tikoo ayng een**glesh***

Do you have a guidebook to the cathedral? Tem um
folheto desta catedral?
*tayng oom fool-**yetoo deshtuh katuh-dral***

I need an English-Portuguese dictionary Preciso de um
dicionário de inglês-português
*pre-**see**zoo doom deess-yoo**nar**-yoo deen**glesh**-poortoo-**gesh***

See also BUYING, NUMBERS, PAYING

a litre of ...
um litro de ...
*oom **leet**roo duh ...*

a kilo of ...
um quilo de ...
*oom **kee**loo duh ...*

100 grammes of ...
cem gramas de ...
*sayng **grah**-mush duh ...*

half a kilo of ...
meio quilo de ...
*mayoo **kee**loo duh ...*

a half-bottle of ...
meia garrafa de ...
mayuh garrah-fuh duh ...

a slice of ...
uma fatia de ...
oomuh fatee-uh duh ...

a portion of ...
um bocado de ...
oom bookah-doo duh ...

a dozen ...
uma dúzia de ...
oomuh doozee-uh duh ...

1000 escudos worth (of) ...
mil escudos de ...
meel shkoodoosh duh ...

a third
um terço
*oom **tehr**-soo*

two thirds
dois terços
*doysh **tehr**-soosh*

a quarter
um quarto
*oom **kwar**too*

three quarters
três quartos
*traysh **kwar**toosh*

ten per cent
dez por cento
*desh poor **sen**too*

more ...
mais ...
mysh ...

less ...
menos ...
***may**-noosh ...*

enough ...
bastante ...
*bash-**tant** ...*

double
o dobro
*oo **doh**-broo*

twice
duas vezes
*doo-ush **vay**-zush*

three times
três vezes
*traysh **vay**-zush*

See also EATING OUT, FOOD, WINES AND SPIRITS, WINE LIST

Starters - Entradas

Amêijoas à Bulhão pato Mussels with onions and coriander
Camarão cozido Boiled shrimps
Camarão grelhado Grilled shrimps
Cocktail de camarão Shrimp cocktail
Espadarte fumado Smoked swordfish
Hors d'oeuvres Mixed hors d'oeuvres
Melão com presunto Melon and ham
Ostras ao natural Oysters

Soups - Sopas

Açorda à alentejana Bread and fish soup
Caldo verde Shredded cabbage soup
Canja de galinha Clear chicken soup
Creme de cenoura Carrot soup
Creme de marisco Shellfish soup
Sopa de feijão-verde Green bean soup
Sopa de legumes Fresh vegetable soup
Sopa de peixe Fish soup
Sopa de tomate Cream of tomato soup

Fish and Seafood – Peixe e Mariscos

Amêijoas Clams
Bacalhau à brás Cod with onion and potatoes
Bacalhau à lagareiro Mashed potato and oven roasted cod
Bacalhau com todos Cod with potatoes, onion, vegetables and coriander
Besugo na grelha Charcoal-grilled sea bream
Caldeirada Fish stew
Camarão Shrimps
Carapaus assados Roast mackerel
Cherne Black jewfish
Chocos com tinta Cuttlefish cooked in their ink
Espadarte Swordfish
Gambas Prawns
Lagosta Lobster
Lagostim Crayfish
Lavagante A kind of lobster
Linguado frito Fried sole
Lulas Squid
Peixe espada Swordfish
Perceves Barnacles
Pescada cozida Boiled hake
Polvo Octopus
Robalo Rock bass
Rodovalho Turbot
Safio Sea eel
Santola Spider crab
Sapateira A kind of crab
Sardinhas Sardines
Tamboril Frogfish
Truta Trout

Poultry - Aves

Codorniz Quail
Faisão Pheasant
Frango Roast chicken
Galinha Chicken
Pato com laranja Duck in orange sauce
Perdiz Partridge
Peru Turkey

Meat - Carne

Bife Steak
Bitoque Steak, fried eggs and chips
Borrego assado no forno Roast lamb
Cabrito assado Roast kid
Carne de borrego/porco/vaca Lamb/pork/beef
Carne de porco à alentejana Pork, cockles and chips
Chanfana à Bairrada Veal in red wine
Coelho à caçador Rabbit
Cozido à portuguesa Stew with beef, potatoes and vegetables
Escalopes de vitela Veal escalopes
Feijoada à transmontana Red beans and pork
Filetes Sirloin steak
Iscas à portuguesa Beef liver
Leitão Suckling pig
Língua de fricassé Tongue
Lombo de porco Pork loin
Pezinhos de coentrada Pig's trotters in coriander sauce
Rins ao Madeira Kidneys in Madeira wine
Rojões à minhota Fried pork loins in red pepper sauce
Steak au poivre Steak in pepper
Steak com cogumelos Steak with mushrooms
Steak com molho de natas Steak and cream sauce
Tripas à moda do Porto Tripe Porto style
Vitela assada Roast veal
Vitela estufada Stewed veal

Eggs - Ovos

Omeleta de camarão Shrimp omelette
Omeleta de fiambre Cold ham omelette
Omeleta de presunto Gammon omelette
Omeleta de queijo Cheese omelette
Ovos escalfados Poached eggs
Ovos estrelados Fried eggs
Ovos mexidos Scrambled eggs

Rice Dishes - Arroz

Arroz branco Boiled rice
Arroz de ervilhas Rice with peas
Arroz de marisco Shrimps and clams with rice
Arroz à Valenciana A type of paella

Salads - Saladas

Salada de agrião Watercress salad
Salada de alface Lettuce salad
Salada mista Mixed salad
Salada de pepino Cucumber salad
Salada de pimentos Green pepper salad

Cheeses - Queijos

Queijo de Azeitão Soft, smooth cheese
Queijo de Castelo Branco Sheep's milk cheese
Queijo do Pico A soft cheese made from cow's milk
Queijo Rabaçal A fresh, sheep's milk cheese
Queijo Saloio Sheep's milk cheese
Queijo de São Jorge A creamy cheese made from cow's milk
Queijo de Serpa A cheese with a strong smell and taste
Queijo da Serra Delicately flavoured sheep's milk cheese
Queijo da Serra da Gardunha Goat's milk cheese

Desserts - Sobremesas

Arroz doce Rice pudding
Bolo de chocolate Chocolate cake
Gelado Ice cream
Maçãs assadas Baked apples
Mousse de chocolate Chocolate mousse
Pudim de amêndoa Almond pudding
Pudim flan Crème caramel
Pudim de frutas Fruit pudding
Pudim de laranja Orange pudding
Pudim de leite Milk pudding
Tarte de amêndoa Almond tart
Torta de laranja Orange roll
Toucinho do céu Almond and egg roll

Understanding the menu

assado roasted
cozido boiled
estufado braised/stewed
no forno oven-baked
frito fried
fumado smoked
grelhado grilled
panado fried in breadcrumbs
refogado fried in oil with garlic and vinegar

I haven't enough money Não tenho dinheiro suficiente
nowng ten-yoo deen-yay-roo soofeess-yent

Have you any change? Tem troco?
tayng trokoo

Can you change a 100 escudo note? Pode-me trocar cem escudos?
pod-muh trookar sayng shkoodoosh

I'd like to change these traveller's cheques Quero trocar estes traveller cheques
kehroo trookar aysh-tush traveller sheksh

I want to change some escudos into pounds Quero cambiar escudos em libras
kehroo kamb-yar shkoodooz ayng leebrush

What is the rate for sterling/dollars? Qual é o câmbio da libra/do dólar?
kwal e oo kamb-yoo duh leebruh/doo dollar

I'd like to cash a cheque with my Eurocheque card Quero levantar um cheque com o meu cartão Eurocheque
kehroo luh-vantar oom shek kong oo may-oo kartowng ay-oorooshek

Can I get a cash advance with my credit card? Pode-me dar dinheiro adiantado com o cartão de crédito?
pod-muh dar deen-yay-roo adee-antah-doo kong oo kartowng duh kreditoo

I should like to transfer some money from my bank in ... Quero transferir dinheiro do meu banco de ...
kehroo transh-fereer deen-yay-roo doo may-oo bankoo duh ...

bureau de change a casa de câmbio
kah-zuh duh kamb-yoo

cash o dinheiro
deen-yay-roo

cheque book o livro de cheques
leevroo duh sheksh

currency a moeda
moo-ay-duh

exchange rate o câmbio
kamb-yoo

notes as notas
notush

post office os correios
koorayoosh

purse a bolsa
bohl-suh

wallet a carteira
kartay-ruh

See also EATING OUT, ENTERTAINMENT

What is there to do in the evenings? O que há para fazer à noite?
oo kee a paruh fazehr a noyt

Where can we go to see a cabaret? Onde é que há um espectáculo de variedades?
ondee é kee a oom shpe-takooloo duh varee-uh-dah-dush

Are there any good night clubs/discos? Há algumas boites/discotecas boas?
a algoomush bwatsh/deeshkoo-tekush boh-ush

How do we get to the casino? Como se vai para o casino?
koh-moo suh vy pro kazeenoo

Do we need to be members? Precisamos de ser sócios?
pre-seezah-moosh duh sehr soss-yoosh

How much does it cost to get in? Quanto custa o bilhete de entrada?
kwantoo kooshtuh oo beel-yet dayn-trah-duh

We'd like to reserve two seats for tonight Queremos reservar dois lugares para esta noite
kray-moosh ruh-zervar doysh loogarush paruh eshtuh noyt

Is there a bar/a restaurant? Há um bar/um restaurante?
a oom bar/oom rushtoh-rant

What time does the show/concert begin? A que horas começa o espectáculo/o concerto?
uh kee orush koomessuh oo shpe-takooloo/oo konsehr-too

How long does the performance last? Quanto tempo dura o espectáculo?
kwantoo tempoo dooruh oo shpe-takooloo

Which film is on at the cinema? Que filme está hoje no cinema?
kuh feelm shta ohj noo seenay-muh

Can we get there by bus/taxi? Pode-se ir para lá de autocarro/de táxi?
pod-suh eer la dowtoo-karroo/duh taxee

See also ROAD SIGNS

Aberto
Open

Acesso para os comboios
To the trains

Água potável
Drinking water

Aluga-se
For hire, To rent

Alto
Stop

Bilheteira
Ticket office

Caixa
Cash desk

Cave
Basement

Completo
No vacancies

Depósito de bagagem
Left-luggage office

Elevador
Lift

Empurrar/ Empurre
Push

Encerrado
Closed

Entrada
Entrance

Entrada livre
No obligation to buy

Frio
Cold

Fumadores
Smokers, Smoking

Homens
Gentlemen, Gents

Informações
Information, Enquiries

Livre
Free, Vacant

Não funciona
Out of order

Ocupado
Engaged

Privado
Private

Proibida a entrada
Keep out, No entry

Proibido fumar
No smoking

Proibido pisar a relva
Do not walk on the grass

Proibido tomar banho
No bathing

Prova (de vinho)
Sampling (of wine etc)

Puxar/Puxe
Pull

Quartos para alugar
Vacancies

Quente
Hot

Rés-do-chão
Ground floor

Saída
Exit

Saída de emergência
Emergency exit

Saldos
Sale

Senhoras
Ladies

Turismo
Tourist Information Office

Vende-se
For sale

See also MEASUREMENTS AND QUANTITIES

0	zero *zehr-oo*	13	treze *trayz*	50	cinquenta *seenkwentuh*
1	um *oom*	14	catorze *katorz*	60	sessenta *sesentuh*
2	dois *doysh*	15	quinze *keenz*	70	setenta *setentuh*
3	três *traysh*	16	dezasseis *dezuh-saysh*	80	oitenta *oytentuh*
4	quatro *kwatroo*	17	dezassete *dezuh-set*	90	noventa *nooventuh*
5	cinco *seenkoo*	18	dezoito *dezoytoo*	100	cem *sayng*
6	seis *saysh*	19	dezanove *dezuh-nov*	110	cento e dez *sentoo ee desh*
7	sete *set*	20	vinte *veent*	200	duzentos *doozentoosh*
8	oito *oytoo*	21	vinte e um *veentee-oom*	300	trezentos *trezentoosh*
9	nove *nov*	22	vinte e dois *veentee-doysh*	500	quinhentos *keen-yentoosh*
10	dez *desh*	23	vinte e três *veentee-traysh*	1,000	mil *meel*
11	onze *onz*	30	trinta *treentuh*	2,000	dois mil *doysh meel*
12	doze *dohz*	40	quarenta *kwarentuh*	1,000,000	um milhão *oom meel-yowng*

1st	primeiro *preemayroo*	6th	sexto *sesh-too*
2nd	segundo *segoondoo*	7th	sétimo *setimoo*
3rd	terceiro *tersayroo*	8th	oitavo *oytah-voo*
4th	quarto *kwartoo*	9th	nono *noh-noo*
5th	quinto *keentoo*	10th	décimo *dessimoo*

See also COMPLAINTS, EATING OUT, MENUS, PAYING, WINES AND SPIRITS

Do you have a set menu? Tem o prato do dia?
tayng oo prah-too doo dee-uh

We will have the menu at 800 escudos Queremos a ementa de oitocentos escudos
kray-mooz uh eementuh doytoo-sentoosh shkoodoosh

May we see the wine list? Pode-nos mostrar a lista de vinhos?
pod-noosh mooshtrar uh leeshtuh duh veen-yoosh

What do you recommend? O que recomenda?
oo kuh ruh-koomenduh

Is there a local speciality? Há alguma especialidade local?
a algoomuh shpuss-yalee-dahd lookal

How is this dish served? Como é servido este prato?
koh-moo e serveedoo aysht prah-too

What is in this dish? O que é que leva este prato?
oo kee e kuh levuh aysht prah-too

Are the vegetables included? Também tem legumes?
tambayng tayng luh-goomsh

Rare/medium rare/well done, please Mal passado/médio/bem passado, por favor
mal pasah-doo/med-yoo/bayng pasah-doo poor favor

We'd like a dessert/some coffee, please Queremos a sobremesa/café, por favor
kray-mooz uh sobruh-may-zuh/kuh-fe poor favor

bill a conta
kontuh

course o prato
prah-too

cover charge o serviço
serveesoo

meal a refeição
ruh-fay-sowng

order o pedido
puh-deedoo

service o serviço
serveesoo

table a mesa
may-zuh

that one aquele (aquela)
akayl (akeluh)

this one este (esta)
aysht (eshtuh)

waiter o empregado
aym-pruh-gah-doo

waitress a empregada
aym-pruh-gah-duh

See also BUYING, MONEY

Can I have the bill, please? Pode trazer
a conta, por favor?
pod trazehr uh kontuh poor favor

Is service/tax included? O
serviço/imposto está incluído?
oo serveesoo/eemposhtoo shta een-klweedoo

What does that come to? Qual é o total?
kwal e oo tootal

How much is that? Quanto custa aquilo?
kwantoo kooshtuh akeeloo

Do I pay a deposit? Deixo depósito?
day-shoo duh-pozitoo

Can I pay by credit card/cheque? Posso
pagar com o cartão de crédito/um cheque?
possoo pagar kong oo kartowng duh kreditoo/oom shek

Do you accept traveller's cheques?
Aceita traveller cheques?
asaytuh traveller sheksh

You've given me the wrong change
Enganou-se no troco
aynganoh-suh noo trokoo

I'd like a receipt, please Quero um
recibo, por favor
kehroo oom ruh-seeboo poor favor

Can I have an itemized bill? Pode-me
dar uma factura com os artigos
discriminados?
pod-muh dar oomuh fak-tooruh kong ooz artee-goosh deesh-kreemee-nah-doosh

cash desk a caixa *ky-shuh*	
cashier o caixa *ky-shuh*	
charge a despesa *dush-pay-zuh*	
cheaper mais barato *mysh barah-too*	
cheque card o cartão de crédito *kartowng duh kreditoo*	
discount o desconto *dush-kontoo*	
expensive caro *kah-roo*	
in advance adiantado *adee-antah-doo*	
payment o pagamento *paguh-mentoo*	
reduction a redução *ruh-doo-sowng*	
signature a assinatura *asseenuh-tooruh*	
till a caixa registadora *ky-shuh rejeeshtuh-doruh*	

My name is ... Chamo-me ...
shah-moo-muh ...

My date of birth is ... Nasci no dia ...
nash-see noo dee-uh ...

My address is ... A minha morada é ...
uh meen-yuh moorah-duh e ...

I come from Britain/America Sou
britânico/americano
soh bree-tahnikoo/ameree-kah-noo

I live in ... Moro em ...
moh-roo ayng ...

**My passport/driving licence number
is ...** O número do meu passaporte/da
minha carta de condução é ...
*oo noomeroo doo may-oo passuh-
port/duh meen-yuh kartuh duh kondoo-
sowng e ...*

My blood group is ... O meu grupo
sanguíneo é ...
oo may-oo groopoo sangeen-yoo e ...

I work in an office/a factory Trabalho
num escritório/numa fábrica
*trabal-yoo noom shkreetor-yoo/noomuh
fabreekuh*

I am a secretary/manager Sou
secretária/gerente
soh sekruh-tar-yuh/juh-rent

I'm here on holiday/business Estou aqui
de férias/em negócios
*shtoh akee duh fehr-yush/ayng negoss-
yoosh*

There are four of us Somos quatro
soh-moosh kwatroo

My daughter is 6 A minha filha tem seis
anos
*uh meen-yuh feel-yuh tayng sayz ah-
noosh*

blind
cego
say-goo

child
a criança
kree-ansuh

deaf
surdo
soordoo

disabled
deficiente
duh-feess-yent

English
inglês
eenglesh

husband
o marido
mareedoo

Irish
irlandês
eerlandesh

Scottish
escocês
shkoosesh

student
o/a estudante
shtoodant

Welsh
galês
galesh

wife
a mulher
mool-yehr

See also CAR PARTS, DRIVING ABROAD, PAYING

20 litres of 2 star petrol Vinte litros de
gasolina normal
veent leetroosh duh gazoo-leenuh noormal

1000 escudos (worth) of 4 star petrol
Mil escudos de gasolina super
*meel shkoodoosh duh gazoo-leenuh
sooper*

Fill it up please Encha o depósito, por
favor
enshuh oo duh-pozitoo poor favor

Check the oil/the water Veja o óleo/a
água
vejuh oo ol-yoo/uh ahg-wuh

Top up the windscreen washers Veja a
água do depósito do limpa pára-brisas
*vejuh uh ahg-wuh doo duh-pozitoo doo
leempuh paruh-breezush*

Could you clean the windscreen? Pode
limpar o pára-brisas?
pod leempar oo paruh-breezush

A can of oil, please Uma lata de óleo, por
favor
oomuh lah-tuh dol-yoo poor favor

Is there a telephone/a lavatory? Há um
telefone/úma casa de banho?
*a oom tuh-luh-fon/oomuh kah-zuh duh
bahn-yoo*

I'd like to use the car wash Gostaria que
me lavassem o carro
*gooshtuh-ree-uh kuh muh lavassayng oo
karroo*

Can I pay by credit card? Posso pagar
com o cartão de crédito?
*possoo pagar kong oo kartowng duh
kreditoo*

attendant
o empregado
aym-pruh-gah-doo

diesel
o gasóleo
gazol-yoo

distilled water
a água destilada
ahg-wuh dushtee-lah-duh

garage
a garagem
garah-jayng

hose
a mangueira
mangay-ruh

petrol pump
a bomba da
gasolina
bombuh da gazoo-leenuh

petrol station
a bomba de
gasolina
*bombuh duh
gazoo-leenuh*

tyre pressure
a pressão dos
pneus
*presowng doosh
pnay-oosh*

I need a colour/black and white film
Preciso de um rolo de fotografias a cores/a preto e branco
pre-seezoo doom roh-loo duh footoogruh-fee-ush uh korush/uh praytoo ee brankoo

It is for prints/slides É para fotografias/slides
e paruh footoogruh-fee-ush/slydsh

Have you got some flash cubes for this camera? Tem cubo flashes para esta máquina?
tayng kooboo flashush paruh eshtuh makinuh

There's something wrong with my cine-camera Tenho problemas com a minha máquina de filmar
ten-yoo proo-blemush kong uh meen-yuh makinuh duh feelmar

The film/shutter has jammed O filme/o obturador está preso
oo feelm/oo obtooruh-dor shta pray-zoo

The rewind mechanism does not work
A alavanca de rebobinagem não trabalha
uh aluh-vankuh duh ruh-boobee-nah-jayng nowng trabal-yuh

Can you develop this film? Pode-me revelar este filme?
pod-muh ruh-vuh-lar aysht feelm

When will the photos be ready?
Quando é que as fotografias estão prontas?
kwandoo e kee ush footoogruh-fee-ush shtowng prontsh

Can I take photos in here? Posso tirar fotografias aqui?
possoo teerar footoogruh-fee-uz akee

---

cartridge
o rolo
roh-loo

cassette
a cassette
kaset

exposure meter
o fotómetro
foo-tometroo

flash
o flash
flash

flash bulb
a lâmpada de flash
lahmpuh-duh duh flash

lens
a objectiva
ob-jeteevuh

lens cover
a tampa da objectiva
tampuh duh ob-jeteevuh

movie camera
a máquina de filmar
makeenuh duh feelmar

negative
o negativo
nuh-guh-teevoo

reel
o carreto
karetoo

tripod
o tripé
treepe

See also ACCIDENTS, CUSTOMS AND PASSPORTS, EMERGENCIES
Police in Portugal have the power to impose fines for traffic
offences. You should go to the police station and pay the fine
within a week.

We should call the police Devemos
chamar a polícia
duh-vay-moosh shamar uh poolees-yuh

Where is the police station? Onde fica a
esquadra?
onduh feekuh uh shkwadruh

My car has been broken into
Assaltaram-me o carro
assal-tah-rowng-muh oo karroo

I've been robbed Fui roubado
fwee roh-bah-doo

I have had an accident Tive um acidente
teev oom aseedent

How much is the fine? Quanto é a
multa?
kwantoo e uh mooltuh

Can I pay at a police station? Posso
pagar na esquadra?
possoo pagar nuh shkwadruh

I don't have my driving licence on me
Não tenho aqui a minha carta de condução
*nowng ten-yoo akee uh meen-yuh kartuh
duh kondoo-sowng*

I'm very sorry, officer Lamento muito,
senhor guarda
lamentoo mweentoo sun-yor gwarduh

I didn't know the regulations Não
conhecia as regras de trânsito
*nowng koon-yuh-see-uh ush regrush duh
tranzeetoo*

car number
a matrícula do
carro
*ma-treekooluh doo
karroo*

documents
os documentos
dookoo-mentoosh

green card
a carta verde
kartuh vehrd

**insurance
certificate**
a apólice de seguro
*apoleess duh suh-
gooroo*

lawyer
o advogado
advoo-gah-doo

police car
o carro da polícia
*karroo duh
pooleess-yuh*

policeman
o polícia
pooleess-yuh

traffic offence
a transgressão
tranj-gresowng

traffic warden
o polícia de
trânsito
*pooleess-yuh duh
tranzeetoo*

If you only want stamps it's simplest to get them in a tobacconist's (*tabacaria*) or shops displaying the *selos* sign. Portuguese post offices have separate counters for different services. They open at 9 am and close at 7 pm. It is the cheapest place to phone.

How much is a letter to England/America? Quanto custa mandar uma carta para a Inglaterra/a América?
kwantoo kooshtuh mandar oomuh kartuh pra eengluh-terruh/amerikuh

I'd like six stamps for postcards to Great Britain, please Quero seis selos para postais para a Grã-Bretanha, por favor
kehroo saysh seloosh paruh poosh-tysh pra grambruh-tahn-yuh poor favor

Twelve 20 escudo stamps, please Doze selos de vinte escudos, por favor
dohz seloosh duh veent shkoodoosh poor favor

I want to send a telegram to ... Quero mandar um telegrama para ...
kehroo mandar oom tuh-luh-grah-muh paruh ...

When will it arrive? Quando é que chega?
kwandoo e kuh shay-guh

How much will it cost? Quanto custa?
kwantoo kooshtuh

Do I have to fill in a form? Tenho que preencher um impresso?
ten-yoo kuh pree-enshehr oom eempressoo

I'd like to make a telephone call Quero fazer uma chamada
kehroo fazehr oomuh shamah-duh

air mail	via aérea
	vee-uh uh-ehr-yuh
clerk	o funcionário
	foonss-yoonar-yoo
counter	o balcão
	balkowng
express	expresso
	eeshpressoo
money order	o vale postal
	vahl pooshtal
parcel	a encomenda
	aynkoo-menduh
post office	os correios
	koorayoosh
postage	a franquia
	frankee-uh
registered	registado
	ruh-jeesh-tah-doo
reply coupon	o cupão
	koopowng

See also ACCIDENTS, COMPLAINTS, EMERGENCIES, POLICE

Can you help me, please? Pode-me ajudar, por favor?
pod-muh ajoodar poor favor

What is the matter? Qual é o problema?
kwal e oo prooblemuh

I am in trouble Tenho problemas
ten-yoo prooblemush

I don't understand Não compreendo
nowng kompree-endoo

Do you speak English? Fala inglês?
fah-luh eenglesh

Please repeat that Pode repetir isso, por favor?
pod ruh-puh-teer eesoo poor favor

I have run out of money Fiquei sem dinheiro
feekay sayng deen-yay-roo

My son is lost O meu filho perdeu-se
oo may-oo feel-yoo perday-oo-suh

I have lost my way Perdi-me
perdee-muh

I have forgotten my passport Esqueci-me do passaporte
shkuh-see-muh doo passuh-port

Please give me my passport back Por favor, devolva-me o
passaporte
poor favor duh-volvuh-muh oo passuh-port

Where is the British Consulate? Onde fica o Consulado
Británico?
onduh feekuh oo konsoo-lah-doo bree-tahnikoo

In the pronunciation system used in this book, Portuguese sounds are represented by spellings of the nearest possible sound in English. Hence, when you read out the pronunciation - the line in *italics* after each phrase or word - sound the letters as if you were reading an English word. The syllable to be stressed is shown in ***bold italics***. The following notes should help you:

	REMARKS	EXAMPLE	PRONOUNCED
a,e,o	as in *pat, pet, pot*	**pá, pé, pó**	*pa, pe, po*
ah,oh	as in *ma, so*	**maço, dou**	*mah-soo, doh*
ee,oo	as in *tree, too*	**triste, tudo**	*treesht, toodoo*
ay	as in *may*	**medo**	*may-doo*
eh	as in *air*	**aéreo**	*uh-ehr-yoo*
uh	as in *mother*	**que**	*kuh*
j	like *s* in *leisure*	**jejum**	*juh-joong*

There are a number of nasal sounds in Portuguese which are pronounced by letting air out through the nose as well as the mouth as in French:

	REMARKS	EXAMPLE	PRONOUNCED
ang	as in *angry*	**maçã**	*masang*
ayng	like *mine*	**mãe**	*myng*
ayng	like *main*	**homem**	*omayng*
eeng	midway between *mean* and *Ming*	**mim**	*meeng*
ong	as in *Hong Kong*	**com**	*kong*
oong	midway between *goon* and *gong*	**algum**	*al-goong*
owng	like *town*	**tão**	*towng*
oyng	like *oi* in *point*	**põe**	*poyng*

Pronouncing Portuguese words from their spelling is not easy as it is a 'flowing' language in which the sounds change depending on the way in which words are joined together. The following rules will help:

	REMARKS	EXAMPLE	PRONOUNCED
ç	as in *facile*	**faço**	*fah-soo*
ch	as in *shampoo*	**champô**	*shampoh*
h	always silent	**homem**	*omayng*
lh	like *lli* in *million*	**milhão**	*meel-yowng*
nh	like *ni* in *opinion*	**pinha**	*peen-yuh*

National Saints' days are public holidays. Each city and the main towns have their own municipal holiday.

New Year's Day	January 1st
Good Friday	April 20th
Freedom Day	April 25th
Labour Day	May 1st
Portuguese National Holiday	June 10th
Corpus Christi	June 21st
Assumption	August 15th
Republic Day	October 5th
All Saints' Day	November 1st
Restoration of Independence	December 1st
Immaculate Conception	December 8th
Christmas Day	December 25th

See also LUGGAGE, TRAIN TRAVEL

On main routes it is a good idea to reserve your seat in advance.
For overnight travel you can book a sleeper or couchette.
Children under 5 travel free. Smoking is allowed only in the
smoking compartments. There are special long-distance luxury
trains.

What time are the trains to ...? A que
horas partem os comboios para ...?
*uh kee orush partayng oosh komboyoosh
paruh ...*

When is the next train to ...? A que
horas parte o próximo comboio para ...?
*uh kee orush part oo prossimoo komboyoo
paruh ...*

When does it arrive? A que horas chega?
uh kee orush shay-guh

Do I have to change? Tenho que mudar
de comboio?
ten-yoo kuh moodar duh komboyoo

A first/second class single to ... Um
bilhete de primeira/segunda classe para ...
*oom beel-yet duh preemay-ruh/segoonduh
klass paruh ...*

A return to ... Um bilhete de ida e volta
para ...
oom beelyet duh eeduh ee voltuh paruh ...

Is there a supplement to pay? É preciso
pagar um suplemento?
e pre-seezoo pagar oom soopluh-mentoo

I want to reserve a sleeper Quero
reservar uma carruagem-cama
*kehroo ruh-zervar oomuh kar-wah-jayng-
kah-muh*

Which platform for the train to ...? De
que linha parte o comboio para ...?
*duh kuh leen-yuh part oo komboyoo paruh
...*

arrival
a chegada
shuh-gah-duh

buffet
o bufete
boofet

departure
a partida
perteeduh

half fare
meio bilhete
mayoo beel-yet

left-luggage
o depósito de
bagagem
*duh-pozitoo duh
bagah-jayng*

reservation
a reserva
ruh-zehrvuh

ticket office
a bilheteira
beel-yuh-tay-ruh

timetable board
o horário
oh-rar-yoo

waiting room
a sala de espera
*sah-luh duh
shpehruh*

See also ACCIDENTS, BREAKDOWNS, EMERGENCIES

I have broken a glass/the window Parti
um vidro/a janela
*partee oom **veedroo**/uh janeluh*

**There is a hole in my shoe/these
trousers** Tenho um buraco no
sapato/nestas calças
*ten-yoo oom boorah-koo noo sapah-too/
neshtush kalsush*

This is broken/torn Isto está partido/roto
eeshtoo shta parteedoo/roh-too

Can you repair this? Pode arranjar isto?
*pod arran**jar eesh**too*

Can you do it quickly? Pode fazê-lo com
urgência?
*pod fazeh-loo kong oor-**jenss**-yuh*

When can you get it done by? Quando é
que está pronto?
kwandoo e kuh shta pront

I need some adhesive tape/a safety pin
Preciso de fita adesiva/de um alfinete de
dama
*pre-**seezoo** duh **feetuh** aduh-**zee**vuh/doom
alfeenet duh **dah**-muh*

The stitching has come undone Caíu-
me uma malha
kayoo-muh oomuh mal-yuh

Can you reheel these shoes? Pode pôr
uns saltos nestes sapatos?
*pod por oonsh sal-toosh naysh-tush
sapah-toosh*

The door handle has come off O
puxador da porta saiu
*oo pooshuh-**dor** duh **portuh** sa-**yoo***

button	o botão
	bootowng
glue	a cola
	koluh
hammer	o martelo
	marteloo
nail	o prego
	pray-goo
pin	o alfinete
	alfeenet
screw	o parafuso
	paruh-foozoo
screwdriver	a chave de parafusos
	shahv duh paruh-foozoosh
string	o cordel
	koordel
tape	a fita adesiva
	feetuh aduh-zeevuh
temporary	temporário
	tempoo-rar-yoo

See also DRIVING ABROAD, ROAD SIGNS, WEATHER
Seats belts are compulsory when driving in the country or on the motorways, but not in the cities or towns.

Is there a route that avoids the traffic? Há outra estrada para evitar o trânsito?
a oh-truh shtrah-duh paruh eeveetar oo tranzeetoo

Is the traffic heavy on the motorway? Há muito trânsito na autoestrada?
a mweentoo tranzeetoo nuh owtoo-shtrah-duh

What is causing this hold-up? Qual é a causa desta demora?
kwal e uh kowzuh deshtuh duh-moruh

When will the road be clear? Quando é que a estrada vai ficar livre?
kwandoo e kee uh shtrah-duh vy feekar leevruh

Is there a detour? Há um desvio?
a oom duj-vee-oo

Is the road to ... snowed up? A estrada para ... está cheia de neve?
uh shtrah-duh paruh ... shta shayuh duh nev

Is the pass/tunnel open? A passagem/o túnel está livre?
uh pasah-jayng/oo toonel shta leevruh

Do I need chains? Preciso de correntes?
pre-seezoo duh koorentsh

accident	o acidente
	asseedent
black ice	o gelo invisível
	jay-loo eemvee-zeevel
fog	o nevoeiro
	nuvway-roo
frost	a geada
	jee-ah-duh
heavy rain	a chuva torrencial
	shoova toorenss-yal
road conditions	o estado da estrada
	shtah-doo duh shtrah-duh
road works	as obras
	obrush
tailback	a bicha
	beeshuh
traffic jam	o engarrafamento
	ayn-garrah-fuh-mentoo
weather conditions	as condições atmosféricas
	kondee-soynz atmoosh-ferikush

See also DRIVING ABROAD, NOTICES

Acenda as luzes
Switch on headlights

Alfândega
Customs

Atenção
Caution

Autoestrada
Motorway

Centro da cidade
City/Town centre

Circule com velocidade reduzida
Slow

Circule pela direita/esquerda
Keep right/left

Conduza pela direita/esquerda
Drive on the right/left

Cruzamento
Road junction

Curva perigosa
Dangerous bend

Dê prioridade
Give way

Descida perigosa
Steep hill

Desvio
Diversion

Entrada
Way in

Entrada proibida
No entry

Escola
School

Estacionamento
Parking

Estacionamento proibido
No parking

Estrada encerrada ao tráfego
Road closed

Estrada em mau estado
Uneven road surface

Estrada com prioridade
Priority

Estrada sem saída
No through road

Fim da proibição de estacionamento
End of parking restrictions

Passagem de nível
Level crossing

Passagem proibida
No right of way

Pavimento escorregadio
Slippery road

Peões
Pedestrians

Perigo
Danger

Portagem
Toll

Prioridade à direita
Priority to the right

Projecção de gravilha
Loose chippings

Reduza a velocidade
Reduce speed

Saída
Way out

Saída de veículos - não estacionar
Exit - keep clear

Sentido único
One-way street

Veículos pesados
Heavy goods vehicles

Velocidade limitada
Speed limit

See also CLEANING, COMPLAINTS, HOTEL DESK, TELEPHONE

Come in! Entre!
entruh

We'd like breakfast/a bottle of wine in our room
Queremos o pequeno almoço/uma garrafa de vinho no nosso quarto
kray-mooz oo puh-kaynoo almoh-soo/oomuh garrah-fuh duh veen-yoo noo nossoo kwartoo

Put it on my bill Ponha na minha conta
pon-yuh nuh meen-yuh kontuh

I'd like an outside line, please Quero uma chamada para o exterior, por favor
kehroo oomuh shamah-duh pro shtuh-ree-or poor favor

I have lost my key Perdi a minha chave
perdee uh meen-yuh shahv

I have locked myself out of my room Deixei a chave no meu quarto
day-shay uh shahv noo may-oo kwartoo

Where is the socket for my electric razor? Onde está a tomada para a máquina de barbear?
onduh shta uh toomah-duh pra makinuh duh barb-yar

What's the voltage? Qual é a voltagem?
kwal e uh voltah-jayng

I need a hairdryer/an iron Preciso de um secador de cabelo/de um ferro
pre-seezoo doom sekuh-dor duh kabay-loo/doom ferroo

May I have an extra blanket/pillow? Pode-me dar mais um cobertor/uma almofada?
pod-muh dar myze oom koobertor/oomuh almoofah-duh

The TV/radio does not work A televisão/o radio não trabalha
uh tuh-luh-veezowng/oo rahd-yoo nowng trabal-yuh

Please send someone to collect my luggage Por favor, mande alguém para levar a minha bagagem
poor favor mand algayng paruh levar uh meen-yuh bagah-jayng

We are going aboard now Vamos a bordo agora
vah-mooz uh bordoo agoruh

The wind is getting up Está a levantar-se vento
shta uh luh-vantar-suh ventoo

It's blowing hard from the north O vento está a soprar fortemente do norte
oo ventoo shta uh sooprar fortment doo nort

It's flat calm Está muito calmo
shta mweentoo kalmoo

We'll have to use the engine Temos que usar o motor
tay-moosh kee oozar oo mootor

When is the weather forecast? A que horas é o boletim meteorológico?
uh kee oruz e oo booluh-teeng met-yooroo-lojikoo

We'll anchor here for the night Ancoramos aqui para passar a noite
ankoorah-mooz akee paruh pasar uh noyt

Please take my mooring line Por favor, ajude-me a atracar o barco
poor favor ajood-muh uh atrakar oo barkoo

I'm feeling seasick Estou enjoado
shtoh aynj-wah-doo

anchor	a âncora
	ankooruh
boom	a verga
	vehrguh
bow	a proa
	proh-uh
dinghy	o bote
	bot
harbour	o porto
	portoo
jib	a bujarrona
	boo-jaronuh
mast	o mastro
	mashtroo
propeller	a hélice
	eleess
rudder	o leme
	lem
sail	a vela
	veluh
sheet	a escota
	shkotuh
stern	a popa
	poh-puh

We've booked an apartment in the name of ... Reservámos um apartamento em nome de ...
ruh-zer-vamooz oom apartuh-mentoo ayng nom duh ...

Which is the key for the front door? Qual é a chave da porta da frente?
kwal e uh shahv duh portuh duh frent

Please show us around Por favor, mostre-nos o apartamento
poor favor moshtruh-nooz oo apartuh-mentoo

Where is the electricity meter/the water heater? Onde está o contador da electricidade/o esquentador?
onduh shta oo kontuh-dor duh eeletree-seedahd/oo shkentuh-dor

How does the heating/the shower work? Como é que o aquecedor/o chuveiro trabalha?
koh-moo e kee oo akussuh-dor/oo shoovayroo trabal-yuh

Which day does the cleaner come? Em que dia é que a mulher da limpeza vem?
ayng kuh dee-uh e kee uh mool-yehr duh leempay-zuh vayng

Is there any spare bedding? Há alguma roupa de cama extra?
a algoomuh roh-puh duh kah-muh eshtruh

A fuse has blown Rebentou um fusível
ruh-bentoh oom foozeevel

Where can I contact you? Onde é que o posso contactar?
ondee e kee oo possoo kontaktar

bathroom a casa de banho *kah-zuh duh bahn-yoo*	
bedroom o quarto *kwartoo*	
cooker o fogão *foogowng*	
electricity a electricidade *eeletree-see-dahd*	
fridge o frigorífico *freegoo-reefikoo*	
gas o gás *gash*	
heater o aquecedor *akussuh-dor*	
kitchen a cozinha *koozeen-yuh*	
light a luz *loosh*	
living room a sala de estar *sah-luh dushtar*	
sheet o lençol *laynsol*	
toilet a casa de banho *kah-zuh duh bahn-yoo*	

See also BUYING, PAYING

Where is the main shopping area?
Onde fica a zona comercial?
onduh feekuh uh zonuh koomehr-see-al

Where are the big stores? Onde ficam os
grandes armazéns?
onduh feekowng oosh granduz armuh-zaynsh

What time do the shops close? A que
horas fecham as lojas?
uh kee orush feshowng ush lojush

How much does that cost? Quanto custa
aquilo?
kwantoo kooshtuh akeeloo

How much is it per kilo/per metre?
Quanto custa um quilo/um metro?
kwantoo kooshtuh oom keeloo/oom metroo

Can I try it on? Posso experimentar?
possoo shpuh-ree-mentar

Where is the shoe/food department?
Onde fica a secção de sapataria/de
comidas?
onduh feekuh uh seksowng duh sapatuh-ree-uh/duh koomeedush

I'm looking for a gift for my wife
Procuro uma prenda para a minha mulher
prookooroo oomuh prenduh pra meen-yuh mool-yehr

I'm just looking Estou só a ver
shtoh so uh vehr

**Have you anything suitable for a
small boy?** Tem alguma coisa para um
rapazinho?
tayng algoomuh koy-zuh proom rapazeen-yoo

carrier bag
o saco de
plástico
sah-koo duh plash-tikoo

cash desk
a caixa
ky-shuh

changing room
o gabinete de
provas
gabeenet duh provush

closed
fechado
fushah-doo

exit
a saída
sa-eeduh

market
o mercado
merkah-doo

open
aberto
abehrtoo

paper bag
o saco de papel
sah-koo duh papel

shopping bag
o saco das compras
sah-koo dush komprush

stall
a bancada
bankah-duh

window
a janela
janeluh

See also MAPS AND GUIDES, TRIPS AND EXCURSIONS

What is there to see here? O que é que
há para ver aqui?
oo kee e kee a paruh vehr akee

guide book
o roteiro
rootayroo

**Excuse me, how do I get to the
cathedral?** Desculpe, como é que se vai
para a catedral?
*dushkoolp koh-moo e kuh suh vy pra
katuh-dral*

map
o mapa
mah-puh

park
o parque
park

Where is the museum? Onde fica o
museu?
onduh feekuh oo moozayoo

**What time does the guided tour
begin?** A que horas é que a visita guiada
começa?
*uh kee oruz e kee uh veezeetuh ghee-ah-
duh koomessuh*

souvenirs
as lembranças
laym-bransush

street plan
o mapa das ruas
*mah-puh dush
roo-ush*

What time does the museum open? A
que horas é que abre o museu?
uh kee oruz e kee ah-bruh oo moozayoo

trip
a excursão
shkoorsowng

Is the castle open to the public? O
castelo está aberto ao público?
*oo kash-teloo shta abehr-too ow
pooblikoo*

view
a vista
veeshtuh

How much does it cost to get in?
Quanto custa o bilhete de entrada?
*kwantoo kooshtuh oo beel-yet dayn-trah-
duh*

**Is there a reduction for children/
senior citizens?** Há um desconto para as
crianças/os reformados?
*a oom dush-kontoo prash kree-
ansush/oosh ruh-foormah-doosh*

Can we take photographs in here?
Podemos tirar fotografias aqui?
*pooday-moosh teerar footoogruh-fee-uz
akee*

The sign for no smoking is *Proibido fumar*. Smoking is forbidden in cinemas, in theatres and on buses.

Do you mind if I smoke? Importa-se se eu fumar?
eemportuh-suh see ay-oo foomar

May I have an ashtray? Pode-me dar um cinzeiro?
pod-muh dar oom seenzay-roo

Is this a no-smoking area? Esta zona é para não-fumadores?
eshtuh zonuh e paruh nowng-foomuh-dorush

A packet of ... please Um maço de ... por favor
oom mah-soo duh ... poor favor

Have you got any American/English brands? Tem algumas marcas americanas/inglesas?
tayng algoomush markuz ameree-kah-nush/eenglay-zush

I'd like some pipe tobacco Quero tabaco para o cachimbo
kehroo tabah-koo pro kasheemboo

Do you have any matches/pipe cleaners? Tem fósforos/limpa-cachimbos?
tayng fosh-fooroosh/leempuh-kasheemboosh

Have you a gas refill for my lighter? Tem uma carga para este isqueiro?
tayng oomuh karguh paruh aysht eeshkay-roo

Have you got a light? Tem lume?
tayng loom

box of matches
a caixa de fósforos
ky-shuh duh foshfooroosh

cigar
o charuto
sharootoo

cigarette papers
as mortalhas
moortal-yush

filter-tipped
com filtro
kong feeltroo

pipe
o cachimbo
kasheemboo

without filter
sem filtro
sayng feeltroo

See also BEACH, ENTERTAINMENT, SAILING, WATERSPORTS

Which sports activities are available here? Que actividades desportivas se podem fazer aqui?
kuh ateevee-dah-dush dushpoor-teevush suh podayng fazehr akee

Is it possible to go fishing/riding? Pode-se ir pescar/andar a cavalo?
pod-suh eer pushkar/andar uh kavah-loo

Where can we play tennis/golf? Onde podemos jogar ténis/golfe?
onduh pooday-moosh joogar tay-neesh/golf

Is there a swimming pool? Há uma piscina?
a oomuh peesh-seenuh

Are there any interesting walks nearby? Vale a pena dar alguns passeios por aqui?
val uh pay-nuh dar algoonsh pa-sayoosh poor akee

Can we rent the equipment? Podemos alugar o equipamento?
pooday-mooz aloogar oo eekeepuh-mentoo

How much does it cost per hour? Quanto custa à hora?
kwantoo kooshtuh a oruh

Do we need to be members? Temos que ser sócios?
tay-moosh kuh sehr soss-yoosh

Where do we buy our tickets? Onde compramos os bilhetes?
onduh komprah-mooz ooj beel-yetsh

Can we take lessons? Podemos ter lições?
pooday-moosh tehr lee-soynsh

ball
a bola
boluh

climbing
o alpinismo
alpee-neejmoo

cycling
o ciclismo
seekleejmoo

gym shoes
os ténis
tay-neesh

gymnasium
o ginásio
jeenaz-yoo

hill-walking
o montanhismo
montan-yeejmoo

pony-trekking
o passeio a cavalo
pasayoo uh kavah-loo

racket
a raqueta
raketuh

shorts
os calções
kalsoynsh

squash
o squash
shkwosh

swimming
a natação
nata-sowng

adhesive tape
a fita cola
feetuh koluh

biro
a esferográfica
shferoo-grafikuh

birthday card
o cartão de anos
kartowng dah-noosh

book
o livro
leevroo

coloured pencils
os lápis de cor
lapeesh duh kor

crayons
os lápis de cera
lapeesh duh sehruh

drawing book
o caderno de desenho
kadehrnoo duh duh-zayn-yoo

envelopes
os envelopes
aym-vuh-lopsh

felt-tip pen
a caneta de ponta de feltro
kanetuh duh pontuh duh feltroo

file
o arquivo
arkeevoo

glue
a cola
koluh

ink
a tinta
teentuh

ink cartridge
a carga para a caneta
karguh pra kanetuh

luggage tag
a etiqueta de bagagem
etee-ketuh duh bagah-jayng

magazine
a revista
ruh-veeshtuh

newspaper
o jornal
joornal

note pad
o bloco de notas
blokoo duh notush

painting book
o livro para pintar
leevroo paruh peentar

paints
as tintas
teentush

paper
o papel
papel

paperback
o livro brochado
leevroo brooshah-doo

paperclip
o clipe
kleep

pen
a caneta
kanetuh

pencil
o lápis
lapeesh

pencil sharpener
o apara-lápis
aparuh-lapeesh

postcard
o postal
pooshtal

refill (for biro)
a carga de esferográfica
karguh duh shferoo-grafikuh

rubber
a borracha
boorah-shuh

stapler
o agrafador
agrafuh-dor

staples
os agrafos
agrah-foosh

writing paper
o papel de carta
papel duh kartuh

You can either hail a taxi or pick one up at a stand. Make sure that the meter is on: if not, ask the price beforehand. Taxis are green and black in Portugal. Tip if you want from 30 to 60 escudos.

Can you order me a taxi? Pode chamar-me um táxi?
pod shamar-muh oom taxee

To the main station/airport, please Para a estação principal/o aeroporto, por favor
pra shtasowng preenseepal/oo uh-ehroo-portoo poor favor

Take me to this address Leve-me a esta morada
lev-muh uh eshtuh moorah-duh

Is it far? É longe?
e lonj

How much will it cost? Quanto custa?
kwantoo kooshtuh

I'm in a hurry Tenho pressa
ten-yoo pressuh

Can you wait here for a few minutes? Pode esperar aqui uns minutos?
pod shpuh-rar akee oonj meenootoosh

Turn left/right here Vire à esquerda/à direita aqui
veer a shkehrduh/a deeraytuh akee

How much is it? Quanto é?
kwantoo e

It's more than on the meter Isso é mais dinheiro do que o que está no contador
eesoo e mysh deen-yay-roo doo kee oo kuh shta noo kontuh-dor

Keep the change Guarde o troco
gward oo trokoo

Make it 300 escudos Arredonde para trezentos escudos
arruh-dond paruh truh-zentoosh shkoodoosh

Can you give me a receipt? Pode-me dar um recibo?
pod-muh dar oom ruh-seeboo

The cheapest way to phone is from the post office or use a phone box. You will pay more if you phone from a restaurant or bar.

I want to make a phone call Quero fazer uma chamada
kehroo fazehr oomuh shamah-duh

Can I have a line? Posso ligar?
possoo leegar

The number is 345 56 78 O número é três quatro cinco, cinco seis, sete oito
oo noomeroo e traysh kwatroo seenkoo seenkoo saysh set oytoo

I want to reverse the charges Quero que seja pagável no destino
kehroo kuh sejuh pagah-vel noo dushteenoo

Have you got change for the phone? Tem dinheiro trocado para o telefone?
tayng deen-yay-roo trookah-doo pro tuh-luh-fon

What coins do I need? De que moedas preciso?
duh kuh mway-dush pre-seezoo

How much is it to phone Britain/the USA? Quanto custa telefonar para a Grã-Bretanha/para os Estados-Unidos?
kwantoo kooshtuh tuh-luh-foonar pra grambruh-tahn-yuh/prosh shtah-dooz-ooneedoosh

I can't get through Não consigo fazer a ligação
nowng konseegoo fazehr uh leeguh-sowng

The line's engaged Está impedido
shta eempuh-deedoo

crossed line as linhas cruzadas
leen-yush kroozah-dush

dialling code o indicativo
eendeekuh-teevoo

dialling tone o sinal de marcação
seenal duh markuh-sowng

directory a lista telefónica
leeshtuh tuh-luh-fonikuh

extension a extensão
eeshten-sowng

operator a telefonista
tuh-luh-fooneeshtuh

phone box a cabine telefónica
kabeen tuh-luh-fonikuh

receiver o auscultador
owsh-kooltuh-dor

transfer charge call a chamada pagável no destino
shamah-duh pagah-vel noo dushtee-noo

Hello, this is ... Allô, daqui fala ...
aloh dakee fah-luh ...

Can I speak to ...? Posso falar com ...?
possoo falar kong ...

I've been cut off Foi interrompida a ligação
foy eenterom-peeduh uh leeguh-sowng

It's a bad line A ligação está má
uh leeguh-sowng shta ma

YOU MAY HEAR:

Estou a tentar fazer a sua ligação
shtoh uh tentar fazehr uh soo-uh leeguh-sowng
I'm trying to connect you

Consegui a ligação
konsuh-ghee uh leeguh-sowng
I'm putting you through

Não desligue
nowng duj-leeg
Hold the line

Lamento, está impedido
lamentoo shta eempuh-deedoo
I'm sorry, it's engaged

Por favor, volte a tentar mais tarde
poor favor volt uh tentar mysh tard
Please try again later

Quem fala?
kayng fah-luh
Who's calling?

Enganou-se no número
aynga-noh-suh noo noomeroo
Sorry, wrong number

See also NUMBERS

What's the time?	**It's:**
Que horas são?	São :
*kee **o**rush sowng*	*sowng*

8.00	oito horas
	oytoo orush
8.05	oito e cinco
	*oytoo ee **seen**koo*
8.10	oito e dez
	oytoo ee desh
8.15	oito e um quarto
	*oytoo ee oom **kwar**too*
8.20	oito e vinte
	oytoo ee veent
8.25	oito e vinte e cinco
	*oytoo ee **veen**tee **seen**koo*
8.30	oito e meia
	*oytoo ee **may**uh*
8.35	nove menos vinte e cinco
	*nov **may**-noosh **veen**tee **seen**koo*
8.40	nove menos vinte
	*nov **may**-noosh veent*
8.45	nove menos um quarto
	*nov **may**-nooz oom **kwar**too*
8.50	nove menos dez
	*nov **may**-noosh desh*
8.55	nove menos cinco
	*nov **may**-noosh **seen**koo*
12.00	meio-dia (*midday*) ; meia-noite (*midnight*)
	*mayoo-**dee**-uh* *mayuh-**noyt***

You may hear the 24-hour clock:

9.00pm	21.00	vinte e uma horas
		***veen**tee **oo**muh orush*
4.45pm	16.45	dezasseis horas e quarenta e cinco minutos
		*dezuh-**sayz** oruz ee kwarentee **seen**koo*
		*mee**noo**toosh*

What time do you open/close? A que horas é que
abre/fecha?
*uh kee oruz e kee **ah**-bruh/**feshuh***

Do we have time to visit the town? Temos tempo para
visitar a cidade?
*tay-moosh tempoo paruh veezeetar uh see-**dahd***

How long will it take to get there? Quanto tempo demora
a chegar lá?
*kwantoo **tem**poo duh-**mor**uh uh shuh-**gar** la*

We can be there in half an hour Chegamos lá em meia hora
*shuh-**gah**-moosh la ayng **may**uh oruh*

We arrived early/late Chegámos cedo/tarde
*shuh-**ga**moosh **say**-doo/tard*

We should have been there two hours ago Devíamos ter
chegado há duas horas
*duh-**vee**-amoosh tehr shuh-**gah**-doo a **doo**-uz orush*

We must be back at the hotel before 11 o'clock Devemos
regressar ao hotel antes das onze
*duh-**vay**-moosh ruh-gre**ssar** ow oh-**tel** antsh duz onz*

When does the coach leave in the morning? A que horas
parte o autocarro de manhã
*uh kee orush part oo owtoo-**karr**oo duh man-**yang***

The tour starts at about half past three A excursão
começa por volta das três e meia
*uh shkoor-**sowng** koomessuh poor **vol**tuh dush trayz ee
mayuh*

The museum is open in the morning/afternoon O
museu está aberto de manhã/de tarde
*oo moozay-oo shta **abehr**-too duh man-**yang**/duh tard*

The table is booked for 8.30 this evening A mesa está
reservada para as oito e meia da noite
*uh **may**-zuh shta rezehr-**vah**-duh praz **oy**too ee **may**uh duh
noyt*

See also EATING OUT, HOTELS, TAXIS

You tip usherettes, taxi-drivers, porters, waiters, toilet attendants, staff in the barber shops, hairdressers, etc. The tip ranges from 50 to 100 escudos.

Sorry, I don't have any change Desculpe, mas não tenho troco
*dush**koolp** mush nowng **ten**-yoo trokoo*

Could you give me change of ...? Podia trocar-me ...?
*poo**dee**-uh troo**kar**-muh ...*

Is it usual to tip ...? É costume dar ...?
*e koosh-**toom** dar ...*

How much should I tip? Quanto é que devo dar?
*kwantoo e kuh **devoo** dar*

Is the tip included? A gorjeta está incluída?
*uh goor-**jetuh** shta een**klwee**duh*

Keep the change Guarde o troco
*gward oo **trokoo***

aftershave
o aftershave
aftershave

baby wipes
os toalhetes
refrescantes
too-al-yetsh
rufresh-kantsh

cleansing cream
o creme de limpeza
krem duh leempay-
zuh

contact lens
cleaner
o líquido para as
lentes de contacto
leekidoo prash
lentsh duh
kontaktoo

cotton wool
o algodão
algoo-downg

deodorant
o desodorizante
duz-oh-doo-
reezant

emery board
a lixa das unhas
leeshuh duz oon-
yush

eye liner
o eye liner
eye liner

eye shadow
a sombra
sombruh

eyebrow pencil
o lápis para as
sobrancelhas
lapeesh prash soh-
bransel-yush

face cloth
o toalhete de rosto
too-al-yet duh
roshtoo

hand cream
o creme para as
mãos
krem prash mownsh

lipstick
o bâton
bah-tong

mascara
o rímel
reemel

moisturizer
o creme hidratante
krem eedra-tant

nail file
a lima das unhas
leemuh duz oon-
yush

nail polish
o verniz das unhas
verneesh duz oon-
yush

nail polish
remover
a acetona
assuh-tonuh

nailbrush
a escova das unhas
shkovuh duz oon-
yush

perfume
o perfume
perfoom

razor
a máquina de
barbear
makinuh duh
barbee-ar

razor blades
as lâminas de
barbear
lah-minush duh
barbee-ar

shampoo
o shampô
shampoh

shaving cream
o creme de barbear
krem duh barbee-ar

soap
o sabonete
saboonet

sponge
a esponja
shponjuh

sponge bag
a bolsa de toilete
bohlsuh duh twalet

suntan cream
o creme
bronzeador
krem bronzee-uh-dor

talc
o pó de talco
po duh talkoo

tissues
os lenços de papel
lensoosh duh papel

toilet water
a água de toilete
ahg-wuh duh
twalet

toothbrush
a escova de dentes
shkovuh duh
dentsh

toothpaste
a pasta de dentes
pashtuh duh
dentsh

TOILETS

In Portugal you will have to pay in public toilets. It's customary to use the toilets in the cafés and bars and tip the attendant, if there is one.

Where is the Gents'/the Ladies'? Onde é a casa de banho dos homens/das senhoras?
onduh shta uh kah-zuh duh bahn-yoo dooz omaynsh/dush sun-yorush

Do you have to pay? Tem que se pagar?
tayng kuh suh pagar

This toilet does not flush O autoclismo não trabalha
oo owtoo-kleej-moo nowng trabal-yuh

There is no toilet paper/soap Não há papel higiénico/sabonete
nowng a papel eej-yenikoo/saboonet

Do I have to pay extra to use the washbasin? Tenho que pagar extra para usar o lavatório?
ten-yoo kuh pagar eshtruh paruh oozar oo lavuh-tor-yoo

Is there a toilet for the disabled? Há casa de banho para deficientes?
a kah-zuh duh bahn-yoo paruh duh-feess-yentsh

Are there facilities for mothers with babies? Há instalações para mães com bebés?
a een-shtalluh-soynsh paruh mynsh kong bebesh

The towels have run out Já não há toalhas
jah nowng a too-al-yush

The door will not close A porta não se fecha
uh portuh nowng suh feshuh

attendant
a funcionária
foonss-yoonar-yuh

contraceptives
os contraceptivos
kontruh-septeevoosh

mirror
o espelho
shpel-yoo

sanitary towels
os pensos higiénicos
pensooz eej-yenikoosh

seat
o assento
asentoo

tampons
os tampões
tampoynsh

vending machine
a máquina de venda automática
makinuh duh venduh owtoo-matikuh

waste bin
o cesto dos papéis
seshtoo doosh papaysh

See also LUGGAGE, RAILWAY STATION

Is this the train for ...? É este o comboio
para ...?
e aysht oo komboyoo paruh ...

Is this seat free? Este lugar está vago?
aysht loogar shta vah-goo

I have a seat reservation Eu tenho um
lugar marcado
ay-oo ten-yoo oom loogar markah-doo

**Can you help me put my suitcase in
the luggage rack?** Pode ajudar-me a pôr
a mala na rede?
*pod ajoodar-muh uh por uh mah-luh nuh
red*

May I open the window? Posso abrir a
janela?
possoo abreer uh janeluh

What time do we get to ...? A que horas
chegamos a ...?
uh kee orush shuh-gah-mooz uh ...

Do we stop at ...? Paramos em ...?
parah-mooz ayng ...

Where do I change for ...? Onde é que
mudo para ...?
ondee e kuh moodoo paruh ...

Is there a buffet car/restaurant car?
Há um bar/um vagão restaurante?
a oom bar/oom vagowng rushtoh-rant

Please tell me when we get to ... Por
favor, diga-me quando chegarmos a ...
*poor favor deeguh-muh kwandoo shuh-
gahr-mooz uh ...*

alarm	o alarme *alarm*
compartment	a carruagem *kar-wah-jayng*
corridor	o corredor *koorruh-dor*
couchette	a couchette *kooshet*
driver	o maquinista *makee-neeshtuh*
express	o expresso *eesh-pressoo*
sleeping car	a carruagem-cama *kar-wah-jayng kah-muh*
ticket collector	o revisor *ruh-veezor*
toilet	a casa de banho *kah-zuh duh bahn-yoo*

What's the best way to get to ...? Qual é o melhor caminho
para ...?
kwal e oo mel-yor kameen-yoo paruh ...

How much is it to fly to ...? Quanto custa um voo para ...?
kwantoo kooshtuh oom voh-oo paruh ...

Are there any special cheap fares? Há alguns bilhetes
especiais mais baratos?
a algoonsh beel-yetsh shpussee-ysh mysh barah-toosh

What times are the trains/flights? A que horas são os
comboios/os voos?
uh kee orush sowng oosh komboyoosh/oosh voh-oosh

Can I buy the tickets here? Posso comprar os bilhetes aqui?
possoo komprar oos beel-yetz akee

Can I change my booking? Posso alterar a minha marcação?
possoo alterar uh meen-yuh markuh-sowng

Can you book me on the London flight? Pode marcar-me
passagem para o voo de Londres?
pod markar-muh pasah-jayng pro voh-oo duh londrush

Can I get back to Manchester tonight? Posso regressar a
Manchester esta noite?
possoo ruh-gruh-sar uh Manchester eshtuh noyt

Two second class returns to ... Dois bilhetes de ida e volta em
segunda classe para ...
*doysh beel-yetsh deeduh ee voltuh ayng segoonduh klass
paruh ...*

Can you book me into a hotel? Pode reservar-me um hotel?
pod ruh-zer-var-muh oom oh-tel

Do you do bookings for shows/concerts? Faz reservas para
espectáculos/concertos?
fash ruh-zehr-vush paruh shpe-takooloosh/konsehr-toosh

A ticket for tonight's performance, please Um bilhete para
o espectáculo desta noite, por favor
oom beel-yet pro shpe-takooloo deshtuh noyt poor favor

See also SIGHTSEEING

Are there any sightseeing tours? Há excursões guiadas?
a skoor-soynsh ghee-ah-dush

When is the bus tour of the town? Quando é a visita guiada à cidade?
kwandoo e uh veezeetuh ghee-ah-duh a seedahd

How long does the tour take? Quanto tempo demora a visita?
kwantoo tempoo duh-moruh uh veezeetuh

Are there any boat trips on the river/lake? Há passeios de barco no rio/lago?
a pasayoosh duh barkoo noo ree-oo/lah-goo

Are there any guided tours of the cathedral? Há algumas visitas guiadas à catedral?
a algoomush veezeetush ghee-ah-duz a katuh-dral

Is there a reduction for a group? Há desconto para grupos?
a dush-kontoo paruh groopoosh

Is there a reduction for senior citizens? Há desconto para reformados?
a dush-kontoo paruh refoormah-doosh

Where do we stop for lunch? Onde paramos para almoçar?
onduh parah-moosh paruh almoosar

Please stop the bus, my child is feeling sick! Por favor, pare o autocarro, o meu filho está enjoado
poor favor pahr oo owtoo-karroo oo may-oo feel-yoo shta aynj-wah-doo

coach trip a viagem de autocarro
vee-ah-jayng dowtoo-karroo

excursion a excursão
shkoorsowng

fare o preço
pray-soo

organized organizado
organee-zah-doo

party a festa
feshtuh

ticket o bilhete
beel-yet

visit a visita
veezeetuh

zoo o jardim zoológico
jardeeng zoh-oolojikoo

bottle opener
o abre-garrafas
abruh-garah-fush

broom
a vassoura
vasoh-ruh

can opener
o abre-latas
abruh-lah-tush

chair
a cadeira
kaday-ruh

cloth
o tecido
tuh-seedoo

clothespeg
a mola
moluh

coat hanger
o cabide
kabeed

comb
o pente
pent

contact lenses
as lentes de
contacto
*lentsh duh
kontaktoo*

corkscrew
o saca-rolhas
sakuh-rol-yush

dish
o prato
prah-too

elastic band
o elástico
eelash-tikoo

flask
o termo
tehrmoo

fork
o garfo
garfoo

frying pan
a frigideira
freejee-day-ruh

glasses
os óculos
okooloosh

hairbrush
a escova de cabelo
*shkovuh duh
kabay-loo*

hairgrip
o gancho de cabelo
*ganshoo duh
kabay-loo*

handkerchief
o lenço
lensoo

knife
a faca
fah-kuh

**needle and
thread**
a agulha e a linha
*uh agool-yuh ee uh
leen-yuh*

penknife
o canivete
kaneevet

plate
o prato
prah-too

plug
a ficha
feeshuh

rope
a corda
korduh

safety pin
o alfinete de
segurança
*alfeenet duh suh-
goo-ransuh*

saucepan
a panela
paneluh

scissors
a tesoura
tuh-zoh-ruh

spoon
a colher
kool-yehr

torch
a lanterna
lantehr-nuh

umbrella
o guarda-chuva
gwarduh-shoovuh

vacuum cleaner
o aspirador
ash-peeruh-dor

**washing-up
liquid**
o detergente
duh-ter-jent

See also BEACH, SAILING

Is it possible to go water-skiing/wind-surfing? É possível fazer ski/wind-surf?
e poo-seevel fazehr shkee/windsurf

Can we rent a motor boat? Podemos alugar um barco a motor?
pooday-mooz aloogar oom barkoo uh mootor

Can I rent a sailboard? Posso alugar uma prancha?
possoo aloogar oomuh pranshuh

Can one swim in the river? Pode-se nadar no rio?
pod-suh nadar noo ree-oo

Can we fish here? Podemos pescar aqui?
pooday-moosh pushkar akee

Is there a paddling pool for the children? Há uma piscina para crianças?
a ocmuh peesh-seenuh paruh kree-ansush

Do you give lessons? Dá lições?
da lee-soynsh

Where is the municipal swimming pool? Onde é a piscina municipal?
ondee e uh peesh-seenuh mooneesee-pal

Is the pool heated? A piscina é aquecida?
uh peesh-seenuh e akuh-seeduh

Is it an outdoor pool? A piscina é descoberta?
uh peesh-seenuh e dushkoo-behr-tuh

canoe
a canoa
kanoh-uh

flippers
as barbatanas
barbuh-tah-nush

goggles
os óculos de protecção
okooloosh duh prootesowng

life jacket
o colete de salvação
koolet duh salvuh-sowng

oar
o remo
ray-moo

rowing boat
o barco a remos
barkoo uh ray-moosh

scuba-diving
o escafandrismo
shkafan-dreejmoo

snorkel
o respirador
rushpeeruh-dor

swimsuit
o fato de banho
fah-too duh bahn-yoo

wetsuit
o fato de mergulhador
fah-too duh mergool-yuh-dor

It's a lovely day Está um dia lindo
*shta oom **dee**-uh **leen**doo*

What dreadful weather! Que tempo horrível!
*kuh **tempoo** oh-**reevl***

It is raining/snowing Está a chover/nevar
*shta uh shoo**vehr**/nuh-**var***

It's windy/foggy Está vento/nevoeiro
*shta **ventoo**/nuv-**wayroo***

There's a nice breeze blowing Sopra um ventinho agradável
*sopruh oom ven**teen**-yoo agruh-**dah**-vel*

Will it be cold tonight? Vai estar frio esta noite?
*vy shtar **free**-oo eshtuh noyt*

Is it going to rain/to snow? Vai chover/nevar?
*vy shoo**vehr**/nuh-**var***

Will there be a frost? Vai cair geada?
*vy kuh-**eer** jee-**ah**-duh*

Will there be a thunderstorm? Vai fazer trovoada?
*vy fa**zehr** troov-**wah**-duh*

Is it going to be fine? Vai estar bom tempo?
*vy shtar bong **tempoo***

Is the weather going to change? O tempo vai mudar?
*oo **tempoo** vy moo**dar***

What is the temperature? Qual é a temperatura?
*kwal e uh temperuh-**too**ruh*

calm	calmo *kalmoo*
clouds	as nuvens *noovaynsh*
cool	fresco *freshkoo*
fog	o nevoeiro *nuv-wayroo*
foggy	enevoado *eenuv-wah-doo*
hot	quente *kent*
mild	ameno *amay-noo*
mist	a neblina *nebleenuh*
misty	nebuloso *neboo-loh-zoo*
sunny	soalheiro *swal-yay-roo*
warm	quente *kent*
wet	húmido *oomidoo*

We'd like an aperitif Queríamos um aperitivo
kree-uh-mooz oom aperuh-teevoo

May I have the wine list, please? Pode-me dar a lista de vinhos, por favor?
pod-muh dar uh leeshtuh duh veen-yoosh poor favor

Can you recommend a good red/ white/rosé wine? Pode recomendar-nos um bom vinho tinto/branco/rosé?
pod ruh-koomendar-nooz oom bong veen-yoo teentoo/brankoo/roh-zay

A bottle/carafe of house wine Uma garrafa/um jarro de vinho da casa
oomuh garrah-fuh/oom jarroo duh veen-yoo duh kah-zuh

A half bottle of ... Meia garrafa de ...
mayuh garrah-fuh duh ...

Would you bring another glass, please? Pode trazer um outro copo, por favor?
pod trazehr oom oh-troo kopoo poor favor

This wine is not chilled O vinho não está fresco
oo veen-yoo nowng shta freshkoo

What liqueurs do you have? Que licores tem?
kuh lee-korush tayng

I'll have a brandy/a Scotch Quero um brandy/um whisky
kehroo oom brandee/oom weeshkee

A gin and tonic Um gin tónico
oom jin tonikoo

A Martini and lemonade Um martini com limonada
oom marteenee kong leemoo-nah-duh

champagne o champanhe
shampan-yuh

dry seco
say-koo

medium meio seco
mayoo say-koo

port o vinho do Porto
veen-yoo doo por-too

sherry o xerez
shuh-resh

sparkling espumoso
shpoomoh-zoo

sweet doce
dohss

vermouth o vermute
vermoot

vodka o vodka
vodkuh

See also EATING OUT, WINES AND SPIRITS

Açores	Region producing the Pico white wines which are dry and fruity
Alentejo	Region producing full-bodied, spicy reds and whites which have a high alcohol content
Algarve	Region producing light, fruity reds and delicate whites with a high alcohol content
Bairrada	Well-balanced, full-bodied red wines and aromatic white wines
Beiras	Light, spicy red wines and sharp, refreshing white wines
Bucelas	Dry white wine which is very acidic when young
Carcavelos	A full-bodied red wine
Colares	Sharp red wines and fruity whites
Dão	Fruity red and white wines
Douro	Region producing Port wine. Port wine can be between 10 and 40 years old. Vintage port is dark and full-bodied. Late Bottled Vintage (L.B.V.) is red and full-bodied. Light white port is sweet
Lafões	Fruity 'green' wines
Madeira	Region producing fortified wines: *Boal* a medium sweet wine; *Malvasia* or *Malmsey* a sweet wine; *Sercial* a dry aperitif; *Verdelho* medium dry wine
Moscatel de Setúbal	A sweet fortified wine from Setúbal
Rosés	These wines are light, slightly dry or sweet and best drunk chilled

Vinho branco	White wine
Vinho da casa/de mesa	House/table wine
Vinho clarete	Light red wine
Vinho comum	Table wine
Vinho doce	Sweet wine
Vinho espumante	Sparkling wine
Vinho espumoso	Sparkling wine
Vinho do Porto	Port wine. See **Douro**
Vinho da região	Local wine
Vinho seco	Dry wine
Vinho tinto	Red wine
Vinho verde	'Green' wine, a semi-sparkling acidic wine best served chilled

The following is a list of all the key words used in this book, with a cross reference to the topic(s) under which they appear. If you don't find the word you are looking for in the wordlist on any given page — look through the phrases.

accelerator → CAR PARTS
accident → ACCIDENTS
activities → SPORTS
address → PERSONAL DETAILS
adhesive tape → REPAIRS, STATIONERY
admission charge → ENTERTAINMENT
adult → FERRIES
advance, in a. → LUGGAGE, PAYING
afternoon → TIME PHRASES
aftershave → TOILETRIES
air mail → POST OFFICE
air-mattress → CAMPING AND CARAVANNING
airport → AIRPORT
alarm → TRAIN TRAVEL
alcohol → CUSTOMS AND PASSPORTS
allowance → CUSTOMS AND PASSPORTS
altar → CHURCH AND WORSHIP
alternator → CAR PARTS
ambulance → ACCIDENTS – INJURIES, EMERGENCIES
America → POST OFFICE
American → SMOKING
anchor, to → SAILING
ankle → BODY
antiseptic → CHEMIST'S
apartment → SELF-CATERING
aperitif → WINES AND SPIRITS
apples → FOOD – FRUIT AND VEG

appointment → BUSINESS, DOCTOR, HAIRDRESSER'S
arm → BODY
armbands → BEACH
arrival → RAILWAY STATION
arrive, to → COACH TRAVEL
ashtray → SMOKING
asparagus → FOOD – FRUIT AND VEG
aspirin → CHEMIST'S
attendant → PETROL STATION, TOILETS
aubergine → FOOD – FRUIT AND VEG
automatic → CAR PARTS
avocado → FOOD – FRUIT AND VEG
avoid, to → ROAD CONDITIONS
baby → CHILDREN
baby food → CHILDREN
babysitter → CHILDREN
babysitting service → CHILDREN
baby wipes → TOILETRIES
back → BODY
bag → LUGGAGE
baggage reclaim → AIRPORT
balcony → ACCOMMODATION
ball → SPORTS
bananas → FOOD – FRUIT AND VEG
bandage → ACCIDENTS – INJURIES, CHEMIST'S
bank → MONEY
baptism → CELEBRATIONS

bar → ENTERTAINMENT, HOTEL
DESK
bathroom → ACCOMMODATION
battery → CAR PARTS
beach → BEACH
beautiful → DESCRIBING THINGS
bed → DOCTOR
bedding → SELF-CATERING
bedroom → SELF-CATERING
beef → FOOD – GENERAL
beer → DRINKS
beetroot → FOOD – FRUIT AND
VEG
begin, to → NIGHTLIFE
beige → COLOURS AND SHAPES
belt → CLOTHES
best wishes → CELEBRATIONS
big → CLOTHES, COLOURS AND
SHAPES
bigger → BUYING
bill → EATING OUT, ORDERING,
PAYING, ROOM SERVICE
biro → STATIONERY
birthday → CELEBRATIONS
birthday card → STATIONERY
bit, a b. → DENTIST
bite, to → ACCIDENTS – INJURIES
bitten → DOCTOR
bitter → DESCRIBING THINGS
black → COLOURS AND SHAPES,
PHOTOGRAPHY
black coffee → DRINKS
black ice → ROAD CONDITIONS
blanket → ROOM SERVICE
bleeding → ACCIDENTS –
INJURIES, DENTIST
blind → PERSONAL DETAILS
blood → CLEANING

blood group → PERSONAL
DETAILS
blood pressure → DOCTOR
blouse → CLOTHES
blow-dry → HAIRDRESSER'S
blue → COLOURS AND SHAPES
boat → BEACH
boat trip → TRIPS AND
EXCURSIONS
body → BODY
bone → BODY
bonnet → CAR PARTS
book → STATIONERY
book of tickets → CITY TRAVEL
book, to → ENTERTAINMENT,
TRAVEL AGENT
booking → HOTEL DESK, TRAVEL
AGENT
booking office
→ ENTERTAINMENT
boot → CAR PARTS
bottle → CHILDREN, WINES AND
SPIRITS
bottle opener → USEFUL ITEMS
bow → SAILING
box of matches → SMOKING
boy → CHILDREN
bra → CLOTHES
bracelet → GIFTS AND
SOUVENIRS
brake fluid → CAR PARTS
brakes → CAR PARTS
brand → SMOKING
brandy → WINES AND SPIRITS
bread → EATING OUT, FOOD –
GENERAL
breakdown van → BREAKDOWNS
breakfast → ACCOMMODATION,
ROOM SERVICE

Catholic → CHURCH AND WORSHIP
cauliflower → FOOD – FRUIT AND VEG
celery → FOOD – FRUIT AND VEG
chains → ROAD CONDITIONS
chair → USEFUL ITEMS
champagne → WINES AND SPIRITS
change → BUYING, MONEY, TAXIS, TELEPHONE
change, to → AIRPORT, BEACH, CHILDREN, CITY TRAVEL, RAILWAY STATION, WEATHER
changing room → SHOPPING
Channel, the → FERRIES
chapel → CHURCH AND WORSHIP
charge → PAYING
chauffeur → CAR HIRE
cheap → TRAVEL AGENT
cheaper → BUYING, PAYING
check, to → PETROL STATION
check in, to → AIRPORT, LUGGAGE
check-in desk → AIRPORT
cheek → BODY
cheers! → CELEBRATIONS
cheese → EATING OUT, FOOD – GENERAL
cheque → PAYING
cheque book → MONEY
cheque card → PAYING
cherries → FOOD – FRUIT AND VEG
chest → BODY
chicken → FOOD – GENERAL
child → PERSONAL DETAILS
children → CHILDREN

chilled → WINES AND SPIRITS
chocolates → GIFTS AND SOUVENIRS
choke → CAR PARTS
christening → CELEBRATIONS
Christmas → CELEBRATIONS
church → CHURCH AND WORSHIP
churchyard → CHURCH AND WORSHIP
cigar → SMOKING
cigarette papers → SMOKING
cigarettes → BUYING
cine-camera → PHOTOGRAPHY
cinema → ENTERTAINMENT
circular → COLOURS AND SHAPES
city → MAPS AND GUIDES
clean → DESCRIBING THINGS
clean, to → CLEANING, PETROL STATION
cleaner → SELF-CATERING
cleansing cream → TOILETRIES
clear → ROAD CONDITIONS
clerk → POST OFFICE
climbing → SPORTS
close → ACCIDENTS – CARS
close, to → SHOPPING, TIME PHRASES
closed → SHOPPING
cloth → USEFUL ITEMS
clothes → CLOTHES
clothespeg → USEFUL ITEMS
clouds → WEATHER
club → ENTERTAINMENT
clutch → CAR PARTS
coach trip → TRIPS AND EXCURSIONS
coastguard → EMERGENCIES
coat → CLOTHES

date of birth → PERSONAL DETAILS
daughter → PERSONAL DETAILS
day → WEATHER
dead → ACCIDENTS – INJURIES
deaf → PERSONAL DETAILS
deck → FERRIES
deck chair → BEACH
declare, to → CUSTOMS AND PASSPORTS
deep → BEACH
denim → CLOTHES
dentist → DENTIST
dentures → DENTIST
deodorant → TOILETRIES
department → BUYING
department store → BUYING
departure → RAILWAY STATION
deposit → PAYING
desk → HOTEL DESK
dessert → EATING OUT
details → BUSINESS
detour → ROAD CONDITIONS
develop, to → PHOTOGRAPHY
diabetic → DOCTOR
dialling code → TELEPHONE
dialling tone → TELEPHONE
diarrhoea → CHEMIST'S, DOCTOR
dictionary → MAPS AND GUIDES
diesel → PETROL STATION
difficult → DESCRIBING THINGS
dinghy → SAILING
dinner → HOTEL DESK
directory → TELEPHONE
dirty → COMPLAINTS, DESCRIBING THINGS
disabled → ACCOMMODATION, PERSONAL DETAILS, TOILETS
disco → NIGHTLIFE

discount → PAYING
dish → ORDERING, USEFUL ITEMS
disinfectant → CLEANING
dislocate, to → ACCIDENTS – INJURIES
disposable nappies → CHILDREN
distilled water → PETROL STATION
distributor → CAR PARTS
dizzy → DOCTOR
doctor → DOCTOR, EMERGENCIES
documents → ACCIDENTS – CARS, POLICE
dollars → MONEY
door → SELF-CATERING
double bed → ACCOMMODATION
double room → ACCOMMODATION
dozen → MEASUREMENTS
drawing book → STATIONERY
dreadful → WEATHER
dress → CLOTHES
drink → EATING OUT
drinking chocolate → DRINKS
drinking water → CAMPING AND CARAVANNING, DRINKS
drive, to → CAR HIRE
driver → CITY TRAVEL, COACH TRAVEL, TRAIN TRAVEL
driving → CAR HIRE
driving licence → ACCIDENTS – CARS, DRIVING ABROAD
dry → WINES AND SPIRITS
dry, to → CLEANING
dry cleaner's → CLEANING
dummy → CHILDREN
duty-free → FERRIES
duty-free shop → AIRPORT

dynamo → CAR PARTS
ear → BODY
earache → DOCTOR
earrings → GIFTS AND SOUVENIRS
easy → DESCRIBING THINGS
eggs → FOOD – GENERAL
elastic band → USEFUL ITEMS
elbow → BODY
electricity → CAMPING AND CARAVANNING
electric razor → ROOM SERVICE
embassy → EMERGENCIES
emergency windscreen → BREAKDOWNS
emery board → TOILETRIES
engaged → TELEPHONE
engine → CAR PARTS, SAILING
England → POST OFFICE
English → PERSONAL DETAILS, PROBLEMS
enjoy, to → CELEBRATIONS
enough → MEASUREMENTS, MONEY
entry visa → CUSTOMS AND PASSPORTS
envelopes → STATIONERY
equipment → SPORTS
escalator → CITY TRAVEL
escudo → MONEY
Eurocheque → MONEY
evening → NIGHTLIFE
evening meal → ACCOMMODATION
excellent → DESCRIBING THINGS
excess luggage → LUGGAGE
exchange rate → MONEY
excursion → TRIPS AND EXCURSIONS

exhaust pipe → CAR PARTS
exhibition → BUSINESS
exit → SHOPPING
expect, to → BUSINESS
expensive → BUYING, PAYING
exposure meter → PHOTOGRAPHY
express → POST OFFICE, TRAIN TRAVEL
extension → TELEPHONE
extra → HOTEL DESK
eye → BODY
eyebrow pencil → TOILETRIES
eye liner → TOILETRIES
eye shadow → TOILETRIES
fabric → CLOTHES
face → BODY
face cloth → TOILETRIES
facilities → CHILDREN, TOILETS
factory → PERSONAL DETAILS
faint, to → DOCTOR
fall → ACCIDENTS – INJURIES
fan belt → CAR PARTS
far → DESCRIBING THINGS, DIRECTIONS
fare → CITY TRAVEL, TRAVEL AGENT, TRIPS AND EXCURSIONS
fast → ACCIDENTS – CARS, DESCRIBING THINGS
fat → COLOURS AND SHAPES
feed, to → CHILDREN
felt-tip pen → STATIONERY
festival → CELEBRATIONS
fetch, to → EMERGENCIES
file → STATIONERY
fill in, to → POST OFFICE
fill up, to → PETROL STATION
filling → DENTIST

film → NIGHTLIFE, PHOTOGRAPHY
film show → COACH TRAVEL
filter → SMOKING
filter-tipped → SMOKING
fine → GREETINGS, POLICE, WEATHER
finger → BODY
fire → EMERGENCIES
fire brigade → EMERGENCIES
first → EATING OUT
first class → RAILWAY STATION
fish → FOOD – GENERAL
fish, to → WATERSPORTS
fishing → SPORTS
flash → PHOTOGRAPHY
flash bulb → PHOTOGRAPHY
flash cube → PHOTOGRAPHY
flask → USEFUL ITEMS
flat tyre → BREAKDOWNS
flaw → COMPLAINTS
flight → AIRPORT
flight bag → LUGGAGE
flippers → WATERSPORTS
flour → FOOD – GENERAL
flowers → GIFTS AND SOUVENIRS
flush, to → TOILETS
fly, to → TRAVEL AGENT
fly sheet → CAMPING AND CARAVANNING
fog → ROAD CONDITIONS, WEATHER
foggy → WEATHER
food poisoning → DOCTOR
foot → BODY
forget, to → EMERGENCIES
forgotten → PROBLEMS
fork → USEFUL ITEMS
form → POST OFFICE

free → TRAIN TRAVEL
French beans → FOOD – FRUIT AND VEG
fridge → SELF-CATERING
fringe → HAIRDRESSER'S
frost → ROAD CONDITIONS, WEATHER
fruit juice → DRINKS
frying pan → USEFUL ITEMS
full board → ACCOMMODATION
fun fair → ENTERTAINMENT
fur → CLOTHES
fuse → CAR PARTS, SELF-CATERING
garage → BREAKDOWNS, PETROL STATION
garlic → FOOD – FRUIT AND VEG
gas → SELF-CATERING
gas cylinder → CAMPING AND CARAVANNING
gas refill → SMOKING
gears → CAR PARTS
Gents' → TOILETS
get in, to → NIGHTLIFE, SIGHTSEEING
get off, to → CITY TRAVEL, COACH TRAVEL
get through, to → TELEPHONE
gift → SHOPPING
gift shop → GIFTS AND SOUVENIRS
gin → WINES AND SPIRITS
girl → CHILDREN
glass → DRINKS, WINES AND SPIRITS
glasses → USEFUL ITEMS
gloves → CLOTHES
glue → REPAIRS
goggles → WATERSPORTS

gold → COLOURS AND SHAPES
golf → SPORTS
good → ASKING QUESTIONS, DESCRIBING THINGS
good afternoon → GREETINGS
goodbye → GREETINGS
good evening → GREETINGS
good morning → GREETINGS
good night → GREETINGS
gown → HAIRDRESSER'S
gramme → BUYING, MEASUREMENTS
grapefruit → FOOD – FRUIT AND VEG
grapes → FOOD – FRUIT AND VEG
green → COLOURS AND SHAPES
green card → ACCIDENTS – CARS, POLICE
grey → COLOURS AND SHAPES
group → TRIPS AND EXCURSIONS
guide book → MAPS AND GUIDES, SIGHTSEEING
guided tour → SIGHTSEEING, TRIPS AND EXCURSIONS
gums → DENTIST
guy rope → CAMPING AND CARAVANNING
gymnasium → SPORTS
gym shoes → SPORTS
hair → HAIRDRESSER'S
hairbrush → USEFUL ITEMS
haircut → HAIRDRESSER'S
hairdryer → ROOM SERVICE
hairgrip → USEFUL ITEMS
hair spray → HAIRDRESSER'S
half-board → ACCOMMODATION
half bottle → WINES AND SPIRITS

half fare → CITY TRAVEL
ham → FOOD – GENERAL
hammer → REPAIRS
hand → BODY
handbrake → CAR PARTS
hand cream → TOILETRIES
handkerchief → USEFUL ITEMS
handle → REPAIRS
hand luggage → LUGGAGE
hand-made → GIFTS AND SOUVENIRS
harbour → SAILING
hard → DESCRIBING THINGS
hat → CLOTHES
hay fever → DOCTOR
hazard lights → BREAKDOWNS
head → BODY
headache → CHEMIST'S, DOCTOR
headlights → CAR PARTS
heart → BODY
heater → SELF-CATERING
heating → SELF-CATERING
heavy → DESCRIBING THINGS, LUGGAGE, ROAD CONDITIONS
heavy rain → ROAD CONDITIONS
hello → GREETINGS
help → EMERGENCIES
help! → EMERGENCIES
help, to → ASKING QUESTIONS, PROBLEMS
high chair → CHILDREN
high tide → BEACH
hill-walking → SPORTS
hire, to → AIRPORT, CAR HIRE
hold, to → TELEPHONE
hold-up → ROAD CONDITIONS
hole → COMPLAINTS
holiday → CELEBRATIONS, CONVERSATION – GENERAL

horrible → DESCRIBING THINGS
hose → CAR PARTS, PETROL STATION
hospital → ACCIDENTS – INJURIES
hot → DESCRIBING THINGS, WEATHER
hotel → AIRPORT, TRAVEL AGENT
hour → TIME PHRASES
house wine → WINES AND SPIRITS
hovercraft → FERRIES
hurry → TAXIS
hurt, to → ACCIDENTS – INJURIES
husband → CAR HIRE, PERSONAL DETAILS
ice → DRINKS
ice-cream → BEACH
ignition → CAR PARTS
ill → DOCTOR
immediately → CLEANING
included → ORDERING, PAYING
indicator → CAR PARTS
inflamed → DOCTOR
information office → DIRECTIONS
injection → DENTIST, DOCTOR
injured → ACCIDENTS – INJURIES
ink → STATIONERY
ink cartridge → STATIONERY
insect bite → CHEMIST'S
insect repellant → CHEMIST'S
insurance certificate → ACCIDENTS – CARS, POLICE
insurance company → ACCIDENTS – CARS

insurance cover → CAR HIRE
interesting → DESCRIBING THINGS
Irish → PERSONAL DETAILS
iron → ROOM SERVICE
iron, to → CLEANING
itemized bill → PAYING
jack → BREAKDOWNS
jacket → CLOTHES
jam → FOOD – GENERAL
jam, to → PHOTOGRAPHY
jazz → ENTERTAINMENT
jeans → CLOTHES
joint → BODY
joint passport → CUSTOMS AND PASSPORTS
jump leads → BREAKDOWNS
keep, to → TAXIS
key → HOTEL DESK
kidney → BODY
kidneys → FOOD – GENERAL
kilo → BUYING, FOOD – GENERAL, MEASUREMENTS, SHOPPING
kilometre → ASKING QUESTIONS
kitchen → SELF-CATERING
knee → BODY
knife → USEFUL ITEMS
lace → CLOTHES
Ladies' → TOILETS
lake → TRIPS AND EXCURSIONS
lamb → FOOD – GENERAL
land, to → AIRPORT
large → CAR HIRE
last, to → NIGHTLIFE
late → HOTEL DESK
later → TELEPHONE
launderette → CLEANING
laundry room → CLEANING

laundry service → CLEANING
lavatory → PETROL STATION
law → ACCIDENTS – CARS
lawyer → ACCIDENTS – CARS,
 POLICE
laxative → CHEMIST'S
layered → HAIRDRESSER'S
leak → BREAKDOWNS
leather → CLOTHES
leave, to → COACH TRAVEL,
 TIME PHRASES
leeks → FOOD – FRUIT AND VEG
left → DIRECTIONS
left-luggage → LUGGAGE,
 RAILWAY STATION
leg → BODY
lemon → COLOURS AND SHAPES,
 FOOD – FRUIT AND VEG
lemonade → DRINKS
lemon tea → DRINKS
lens → PHOTOGRAPHY
lens cover → PHOTOGRAPHY
less → MEASUREMENTS
lessons → SPORTS
letter → POST OFFICE
lettuce → FOOD – FRUIT AND
 VEG
lifeboat → FERRIES
lifeguard → BEACH
life jacket → FERRIES,
 WATERSPORTS
lift → ACCOMMODATION
light → CLOTHES, COLOURS AND
 SHAPES, DESCRIBING THINGS,
 SELF-CATERING, SMOKING
lighter → SMOKING
like, to → CONVERSATION –
 GENERAL
line → TELEPHONE

lipstick → TOILETRIES
liqueur → WINES AND SPIRITS
literature → BUSINESS
litre → FOOD – GENERAL,
 MEASUREMENTS, PETROL
 STATION
live, to → PERSONAL DETAILS
liver → BODY, FOOD – GENERAL
living room → SELF-CATERING
local → MAPS AND GUIDES,
 ORDERING
lock → COMPLAINTS
locked out → ROOM SERVICE
locker → LUGGAGE
long → COLOURS AND SHAPES,
 DESCRIBING THINGS, FERRIES,
 HAIRDRESSER'S
look for, to → SHOPPING
lost → DIRECTIONS
lost property office
 → EMERGENCIES
lotion → CHEMIST'S
lounge → AIRPORT, HOTEL DESK
lovely → DESCRIBING THINGS,
 WEATHER
low tide → BEACH
luggage → LUGGAGE
luggage allowance → LUGGAGE
luggage hold → COACH TRAVEL
luggage rack → LUGGAGE
luggage tag → STATIONERY
luggage trolley → LUGGAGE
lunch → ACCOMMODATION
lung → BODY
magazine → STATIONERY
main → SHOPPING
main course → EATING OUT
major road → DRIVING ABROAD

mallet → CAMPING AND
CARAVANNING
manage, to → LUGGAGE
manager → HOTEL DESK
map → MAPS AND GUIDES
margarine → FOOD – GENERAL
market → SHOPPING
Martini → WINES AND SPIRITS
mascara → TOILETRIES
mass → CHURCH AND WORSHIP
mast → SAILING
matches → SMOKING
material → CLOTHES
mauve → COLOURS AND SHAPES
meal → ORDERING
measure, to → CLOTHES
mechanic → BREAKDOWNS
medicine → DOCTOR
medium → WINES AND SPIRITS
medium rare → ORDERING
melon → FOOD – FRUIT AND VEG
member → NIGHTLIFE
menu → EATING OUT,
ORDERING
message → BUSINESS
meter → SELF-CATERING, TAXIS
metre → SHOPPING
mild → WEATHER
milk → DRINKS, FOOD –
GENERAL
mince → FOOD – GENERAL
mind, to → SMOKING
mineral water → DRINKS
minister → CHURCH AND
WORSHIP
minor road → DRIVING ABROAD
mirror → TOILETS
missing → EMERGENCIES
mist → WEATHER

misty → WEATHER
moisturizer → TOILETRIES
money → MONEY
money order → POST OFFICE
more → GIFTS AND SOUVENIRS,
MEASUREMENTS
morning → TIME PHRASES
mosque → CHURCH AND
WORSHIP
mother → TOILETS
motor boat → WATERSPORTS
motorway → DRIVING ABROAD
mouth → BODY
move, to → ACCIDENTS –
INJURIES
movie camera → PHOTOGRAPHY
municipal → WATERSPORTS
muscle → BODY
museum → SIGHTSEEING
mushrooms → FOOD – FRUIT
AND VEG
mustard → FOOD – GENERAL
nail → REPAIRS
nailbrush → TOILETRIES
nail file → TOILETRIES
nail polish → TOILETRIES
nail polish remover
→ TOILETRIES
name → PERSONAL DETAILS
nappy → CHILDREN
national → CUSTOMS AND
PASSPORTS
near → DESCRIBING THINGS,
DIRECTIONS
nearest → DIRECTIONS
neck → BODY
necklace → GIFTS AND
SOUVENIRS
need, to → DOCTOR

pass → ROAD CONDITIONS
passport → EMERGENCIES, PERSONAL DETAILS
passport control → AIRPORT
pay, to → PAYING
payment → PAYING
peaches → FOOD – FRUIT AND VEG
pears → FOOD – FRUIT AND VEG
peas → FOOD – FRUIT AND VEG
pen → STATIONERY
pencil → STATIONERY
pencil sharpener → STATIONERY
penicillin → DOCTOR
penknife → USEFUL ITEMS
pepper → FOOD – FRUIT AND VEG, FOOD – GENERAL
per → CAMPING AND CARAVANNING
performance → NIGHTLIFE
perfume → TOILETRIES
perm → HAIRDRESSER'S
permed → HAIRDRESSER'S
petrol → BREAKDOWNS, PETROL STATION
petrol pump → PETROL STATION
petrol station → PETROL STATION
petrol tank → BREAKDOWNS
petticoat → CLOTHES
phone → TELEPHONE
phone, to → TELEPHONE
phone box → TELEPHONE
phone call → TELEPHONE
photocopying → BUSINESS
photos → PHOTOGRAPHY
pill → DOCTOR
pin → REPAIRS

pineapple → FOOD – FRUIT AND VEG
pink → COLOURS AND SHAPES
pipe → SMOKING
pipe cleaners → SMOKING
pipe tobacco → SMOKING
plane → AIRPORT
plate → USEFUL ITEMS
platform → RAILWAY STATION
play → ENTERTAINMENT
play, to → ENTERTAINMENT, SPORTS
playroom → CHILDREN
pleasant → DESCRIBING THINGS
plug → USEFUL ITEMS
plums → FOOD – FRUIT AND VEG
pointed → COLOURS AND SHAPES
points → CAR PARTS
poisoning → DOCTOR
police → ACCIDENTS – CARS, POLICE
police car → POLICE
policeman → POLICE
police station → POLICE
polyester → CLOTHES
pony-trekking → SPORTS
pork → FOOD – GENERAL
port → WINES AND SPIRITS
porter → HOTEL DESK, LUGGAGE
portion → MEASUREMENTS
Portugal → CONVERSATION – GENERAL
Portuguese → CONVERSATION – MEETING
possible → SPORTS
postage → POST OFFICE
postcard → STATIONERY
post office → POST OFFICE
pot → DRINKS

potatoes → FOOD – FRUIT AND VEG
pottery → GIFTS AND SOUVENIRS
pound → FOOD – GENERAL
pounds → MONEY
pram → CHILDREN
prefer, to → BUYING
pregnant → DOCTOR
prescription → CHEMIST's
present → GIFTS AND SOUVENIRS
priest → CHURCH AND WORSHIP
prints → PHOTOGRAPHY
private → BEACH
propeller → SAILING
Protestant → CHURCH AND WORSHIP
public → SIGHTSEEING
public holiday → CELEBRATIONS
purple → COLOURS AND SHAPES
purse → MONEY
purser → FERRIES
push chair → CHILDREN
put, to → ROOM SERVICE
put through, to → TELEPHONE
pyjamas → CLOTHES
quarter → MEASUREMENTS
quickly → EMERGENCIES
quiet → BEACH
rabbi → CHURCH AND WORSHIP
racket → SPORTS
radiator → CAR PARTS
radio → CAR HIRE
radio-cassette → CAR HIRE
radishes → FOOD – FRUIT AND VEG
rain, to → WEATHER
raincoat → CLOTHES
rare → ORDERING

raspberries → FOOD – FRUIT AND VEG
rate → MONEY
razor → TOILETRIES
razor blades → TOILETRIES
ready → ASKING QUESTIONS
receipt → PAYING
receiver → TELEPHONE
reclining seat → FERRIES
recommend, to → ORDERING
red → COLOURS AND SHAPES, WINES AND SPIRITS
reduction → PAYING
reel → PHOTOGRAPHY
refill → STATIONERY
regional → GIFTS AND SOUVENIRS
registered → POST OFFICE
regulations → POLICE
reheel, to → REPAIRS
remove, to → CLEANING
rent, to → SPORTS
repair, to → BREAKDOWNS, REPAIRS
repeat, to → PROBLEMS
reply coupon → POST OFFICE
reservation → HOTEL DESK, RAILWAY STATION
reserve, to → AIRPORT, HOTEL DESK, RAILWAY STATION
restaurant → EATING OUT
restaurant car → TRAIN TRAVEL
return → RAILWAY STATION
return ticket → FERRIES
reversing lights → CAR PARTS
rice → FOOD – GENERAL
riding → SPORTS
right → DIRECTIONS
ring → GIFTS AND SOUVENIRS

river → WATERSPORTS
road → DRIVING ABROAD
road conditions → ROAD CONDITIONS
road map → MAPS AND GUIDES
road sign → DIRECTIONS
road works → ROAD CONDITIONS
rob, to → POLICE
room → HOTEL DESK
room service → HOTEL DESK
rope → USEFUL ITEMS
rosé → WINES AND SPIRITS
rough → DESCRIBING THINGS, FERRIES
round → COLOURS AND SHAPES
route → ROAD CONDITIONS
rowing boat → WATERSPORTS
rubber → STATIONERY
rudder → SAILING
run out of, to → BREAKDOWNS, PROBLEMS
safe → BEACH, CHEMIST'S
safety pin → REPAIRS, USEFUL ITEMS
sail → SAILING
sailboard → WATERSPORTS
sailing → FERRIES
salt → FOOD – GENERAL
sample → BUSINESS
sandals → CLOTHES
sandwich → EATING OUT
sanitary towels → CHEMIST'S
saucepan → USEFUL ITEMS
scarf → CLOTHES
scissors → USEFUL ITEMS
Scotch → WINES AND SPIRITS
Scottish → PERSONAL DETAILS
screw → REPAIRS

screwdriver → REPAIRS
scuba-diving → WATERSPORTS
sea → BEACH, FERRIES
seasick → SAILING
season ticket → CITY TRAVEL
seat → COACH TRAVEL, TOILETS, TRAIN TRAVEL
seat belt → DRIVING ABROAD
seat reservation → TRAIN TRAVEL
second class → RAILWAY STATION, TRAVEL AGENT
secretary → BUSINESS
see, to → SIGHTSEEING
sell, to → BUYING
send, to → POST OFFICE
senior citizen → SIGHTSEEING
serious → ACCIDENTS – INJURIES
serve, to → ORDERING
served, to be → COMPLAINTS
service → CHURCH AND WORSHIP, ORDERING
set → HAIRDRESSER'S
set menu → EATING OUT
shade → COLOURS AND SHAPES
shampoo → TOILETRIES
shandy → DRINKS
shaving cream → TOILETRIES
sheet → SELF-CATERING
sherry → WINES AND SPIRITS
shiny → COLOURS AND SHAPES
ship → FERRIES
shirt → CLOTHES
shock absorber → CAR PARTS
shoes → CLOTHES
shop → BUYING
shopping area → SHOPPING
shopping bag → SHOPPING

short → DESCRIBING THINGS, HAIRDRESSER'S
short cut → DRIVING ABROAD
shorts → CLOTHES, SPORTS
shoulder → BODY
show → NIGHTLIFE
show, to → DIRECTIONS, MAPS AND GUIDES
shower → SELF-CATERING
shutter → PHOTOGRAPHY
sick → DOCTOR, TRIPS AND EXCURSIONS
sightseeing → TRIPS AND EXCURSIONS
sign → DRIVING ABROAD
signature → PAYING
silk → CLOTHES
silver → COLOURS AND SHAPES
single → RAILWAY STATION
single bed → ACCOMMODATION
single room → ACCOMMODATION
sink → CLEANING
sit, to → CONVERSATION – MEETING
site → CAMPING AND CARAVANNING
skin → BODY
skirt → CLOTHES
sleep, to → DOCTOR
sleeper → RAILWAY STATION
sleeping bag → CAMPING AND CARAVANNING
sleeping car → TRAIN TRAVEL
slice → MEASUREMENTS
slides → PHOTOGRAPHY
slip, to → ACCIDENTS – INJURIES
slow → DESCRIBING THINGS
small → COLOURS AND SHAPES

smaller → BUYING
smoke, to → SMOKING
smooth → DESCRIBING THINGS, FERRIES
snack bar → AIRPORT
snorkel → WATERSPORTS
snow, to → WEATHER
snowed up → ROAD CONDITIONS
soap → TOILETRIES
socket → ROOM SERVICE
socks → CLOTHES
soft → DESCRIBING THINGS
soft drink → DRINKS
son → CHILDREN
sore → CHEMIST'S, DENTIST, DOCTOR
sorry → CONVERSATION – GENERAL
soup → EATING OUT, FOOD – GENERAL
sour → DESCRIBING THINGS
souvenir → GIFTS AND SOUVENIRS
spade → BEACH
spanner → BREAKDOWNS
spare → SELF-CATERING
sparkling → WINES AND SPIRITS
spark plugs → CAR PARTS
speak, to → CONVERSATION – MEETING, PROBLEMS, TELEPHONE
special → TRAVEL AGENT
special menu → CHILDREN
special rate → CHILDREN
speciality → ORDERING
speed limit → DRIVING ABROAD
spicy → DESCRIBING THINGS
spinach → FOOD – FRUIT AND VEG

sponge → TOILETRIES
sponge bag → TOILETRIES
spoon → USEFUL ITEMS
sports → SPORTS
sprain → ACCIDENTS – INJURIES
square → COLOURS AND SHAPES
squash → SPORTS
stain → CLEANING
stall → SHOPPING
stamps → POST OFFICE
stapler → STATIONERY
staples → STATIONERY
starter → EATING OUT
station → TAXIS
stay → HOTEL DESK
stay, to → DOCTOR
steak → FOOD – GENERAL
steering → CAR PARTS
steering wheel → CAR PARTS
sterling → MONEY
stern → SAILING
sticking plaster → CHEMIST'S
stitching → REPAIRS
stockings → CLOTHES
stolen → EMERGENCIES
stomach → BODY
stomach upset → DOCTOR
stop, to → TRAIN TRAVEL, TRIPS
AND EXCURSIONS
straight → HAIRDRESSER'S
straight on → DIRECTIONS
strawberries → FOOD – FRUIT
AND VEG
streaks → HAIRDRESSER'S
street map → MAPS AND GUIDES
street plan → SIGHTSEEING
string → REPAIRS
strong → DESCRIBING THINGS
student → PERSONAL DETAILS

stung → ACCIDENTS – INJURIES
styling mousse
→ HAIRDRESSER'S
suede → CLOTHES
sugar → FOOD – GENERAL
suit (man's) → CLOTHES
suit (woman's) → CLOTHES
suitable → SHOPPING
suitcase → LUGGAGE
sunburn → ACCIDENTS –
INJURIES
sunglasses → BEACH
sunny → WEATHER
sunshade → BEACH
sunstroke → ACCIDENTS –
INJURIES
suntan cream → TOILETRIES
suntan oil → BEACH
supermarket → BUYING
supplement → RAILWAY
STATION
swallow, to → DOCTOR
sweater → CLOTHES
sweet → DESCRIBING THINGS,
WINES AND SPIRITS
swim, to → BEACH
swimming → SPORTS
swimming pool → SPORTS
swimsuit → BEACH, CLOTHES
synagogue → CHURCH AND
WORSHIP
table → EATING OUT, ORDERING
table linen → GIFTS AND
SOUVENIRS
tablet → DOCTOR
tailback → ROAD CONDITIONS
take, to → CHEMIST'S,
DIRECTIONS. SPORTS
take out, to → DENTIST

take up, to → HOTEL DESK
talc → TOILETRIES
tampons → CHEMIST'S
tap → CLEANING
tape → REPAIRS
tax → PAYING
taxi → TAXIS
tea → DRINKS, FOOD – GENERAL
telegram → POST OFFICE
telephone → PETROL STATION
telex → BUSINESS
tell, to → TRAIN TRAVEL
temperature → DOCTOR, WEATHER
temporary → REPAIRS
tennis → SPORTS
tent → CAMPING AND CARAVANNING
tent peg → CAMPING AND CARAVANNING
tent pole → CAMPING AND CARAVANNING
terrace → EATING OUT
thank you → CONVERSATION – MEETING
that one → ORDERING
theatre → ENTERTAINMENT
thick → COLOURS AND SHAPES
thin → COLOURS AND SHAPES
things → CLEANING
third → MEASUREMENTS
this one → ORDERING
throat → BODY
through → DIRECTIONS
thumb → BODY
thunderstorm → WEATHER
ticket → CITY TRAVEL, ENTERTAINMENT, TRIPS AND EXCURSIONS

ticket collector → TRAIN TRAVEL
ticket office → RAILWAY STATION
tie → CLOTHES
tights → CLOTHES
till → PAYING
time → TIME, TIME PHRASES
timetable board → RAILWAY STATION
tin → FOOD – GENERAL
tinted → COLOURS AND SHAPES
tip, to → TIPPING
tissues → TOILETRIES
tobacco → CUSTOMS AND PASSPORTS
toe → BODY
toilet → TOILETS
toilet paper → TOILETS
toilet water → TOILETRIES
toll → DRIVING ABROAD
tomatoes → FOOD – FRUIT AND VEG
tomorrow → BUSINESS
tongue → BODY
tonight → NIGHTLIFE
too → CLOTHES
tooth → DENTIST
toothache → DENTIST
toothbrush → TOILETRIES
toothpaste → TOILETRIES
torch → USEFUL ITEMS
torn → REPAIRS
tour → TRIPS AND EXCURSIONS
tourist → DIRECTIONS.
tourist office → MAPS AND GUIDES
tourist ticket → CITY TRAVEL
tow, to → BREAKDOWNS
tow rope → BREAKDOWNS

towel → BEACH, HAIRDRESSER'S
town → CITY TRAVEL
town centre → CITY TRAVEL
town plan → MAPS AND GUIDES
trade fair → BUSINESS
traffic → ROAD CONDITIONS
traffic jam → ROAD CONDITIONS
traffic lights → DRIVING
  ABROAD
traffic offence → POLICE
traffic warden → POLICE
trailer → CAMPING AND
  CARAVANNING
train → CITY TRAVEL, TRAIN
  TRAVEL
transfer, to → MONEY
transfer charge call
  → TELEPHONE
transit, in t. → LUGGAGE
travel, to → GIFTS AND
  SOUVENIRS
traveller's cheques → MONEY
trim → HAIRDRESSER'S
trip → SIGHTSEEING
tripod → PHOTOGRAPHY
trouble → PROBLEMS
trousers → CLOTHES
trunk → LUGGAGE
trunks → CLOTHES
try on, to → CLOTHES
t-shirt → CLOTHES
tunnel → ROAD CONDITIONS
turn, to → TAXIS
turn off, to → COMPLAINTS
turn on, to → COMPLAINTS
turning → DIRECTIONS
turquoise → COLOURS AND
  SHAPES
TV lounge → HOTEL DESK

twice → MEASUREMENTS
tyre → CAR PARTS
tyre pressure → PETROL
  STATION
umbrella → USEFUL ITEMS
unconscious → DOCTOR
under → DIRECTIONS
underground → CITY TRAVEL
underground station → CITY
  TRAVEL
understand, to → ASKING
  QUESTIONS
unpleasant → DESCRIBING
  THINGS
upset → CHEMIST'S
urgently → DENTIST
use, to → TOILETS
vacancies → CAMPING AND
  CARAVANNING
vacuum cleaner → USEFUL
  ITEMS
veal → FOOD – GENERAL
vegetables → EATING OUT
vending machine → TOILETS
vermouth → WINES AND SPIRITS
vest → CLOTHES
view → SIGHTSEEING
vinegar → FOOD – GENERAL
visit → TRIPS AND EXCURSIONS
vodka → WINES AND SPIRITS
voltage → ROOM SERVICE
wait, to → TAXIS
waiter → ORDERING
waiting → COMPLAINTS
waiting room → RAILWAY
  STATION
waitress → ORDERING
walk, to → DIRECTIONS
wallet → MONEY